MEATLESS
INDIAN
COOKING
From The Curry Club

How to Order:
Quantity discounts are available from the publisher, Prima Publishing, P.O. Box 1260BK Rocklin, CA 95677; telephone (916) 632-4400. On your letterhead include information concerning the intended use of the books and the number of books you wish to purchase.

MEATLESS INDIAN COOKING

From The Curry Club

Over 150 Delicious Dishes

Pat Chapman

PRIMA PUBLISHING

PRIMA PUBLISHING and its colophon, which consists of the letter P over PRIMA, are trademarks of Prima Communications, Inc.

Cover design by The Dunlavey Studio, Sacramento

Library of Congress Cataloging-in-Publication Data

Chapman, Pat, 1940-
    Meatless Indian cooking from the Curry Club : over 150
delicious dishes / Pat Chapman.
        p.   cm.
    Includes index.
    ISBN 1-55958-690-7
    1. Vegetarian cookery. 2. Cookery, India. I. Title.
TX837.C4515 1995
641.5'636—dc20   94-39442

95 96 97 98 99 RRD 10 9 8 7 6 5 4 3 2 1
Printed in the United States of America

Contents

Introduction

I have an enormous collection of recipes. I collect them as other people collect stamps. They have come from all over the world and particularly, as you might suspect, from those countries where spicy cooking prevails.

I have two main sources. The first is professional cooks – mostly hotel and restaurant chefs who adore talking about food and, given half a chance, demonstrating it as well. My other source is 'ordinary' people.

Everyone is an expert about food. Everyone eats it. And if they don't cook it they certainly know someone who does. It is a wonderful topic of conversation, particularly with people you haven't met before and it can lead to the most extraordinary and generous invitations to private homes and kitchens. When they discover you have a genuine interest in their food, people from any status forget class barriers and social customs. I have chopped onions in the kitchen of a Kashmiri travel agent. He was the strictest Moslem, yet he was so intrigued by my interest in Kashmiri cooking that he persuaded his wife to take me into her kitchen (where no outside man is normally permitted) while she and her daughters cooked the evening meal.

On another occasion, in Bombay, I was invited to a cocktail party. The host was a Sikh and he was an astoundingly wealthy businessman. His apartment was as big as a cricket pitch and his cocktail cabinet contained every drink known to mankind and some more as well. I had attended as a business duty. The conversation was predictably stilted and I wondered how soon I could leave without appearing rude. Then enter the canapés. They were exquisite and beguiling; tiny and tasty, yet typically Indian. Naturally I asked how they were made, expecting an evasive answer about servants. At once the conversation became animated and excited. Leaving his other guests to their own devices, the host whisked me off to the kitchen, which was bigger than most restaurant kitchens I've been in. His wife came too in her $1,000 sari. Within minutes the rock-sized precious-stone rings came off her elegantly manicured hands and she and her husband started rolling out micro samosas and rissoles, shaping weeny kebabs and chattering away about garam masala. The servants stood around amused and amazed, not at their master and mistress, whose antics they were used to, but at me. They couldn't believe I was genuinely interested in the proceedings.

Several hours later everyone including guests, hosts and servants declared it the best party they had been to. A complete meal had been cooked from scratch. Just about everyone had contributed something and many recipes had been exchanged.

I now always make sure I have suitable recipes with me wherever I go. I learned a long time ago that the two most popular English recipes are chocolate cake and Yorkshire pudding. For vegans, who cannot eat eggs and milk, recipes for clear vegetable consommé and vegetable pie are popular. Armed with these and a large notepad and pen, you'll find that you not only learn a fantastic amount, but you'll be giving something as well, and with any luck you'll have a memorable evening, a great meal and make new friends for life. I've had many such chance encounters turn into worthwhile experiences and almost without noticing it one builds up an extraordinary collection of recipes.

Which brings me to this book. A great many people in the curry lands are vegetarian. In India alone around 500 million people are vegetarian and if India's neighbouring ten curry lands are added in, there is a population in excess of 1·2 billion, of which 800 million are vegetarian.

In the last decade or two the fundamentally non vegetarian population of the West have become aware of the shortcomings of meat eating. New vegetarian products have arrived at the supermarkets to cater for this new awareness and the subject of healthy food fills the pages of our media to the point of tedium. Between three and five per cent of the British population are completely vegetarian and there are 18 million demi-vegetarians in the country (that is, people who follow a mostly vegetarian diet but who do eat meat and/or fish occasionally). The number of vegetarian restaurants and restaurants that offer vegetarian alternatives on their menu is growing all the time. Even some schools and office canteens now offer at least one vegetarian dish.

Many of the delightful people I have met on my travels have been vegetarian and my recipe collection reflects this. In fact I was quite surprised by its extent. There was easily enough material to fill a book and to widen the sphere of interest to include vegetarian recipes from the ten curry lands. From west to east they include Afghanistan, Pakistan, the seven main culinary regions of India (Kashmir in the north, the Punjab, Rajahstan, Gujerat, Central, Eastern and Southern India), Nepal, Bangladesh, Sri Lanka, Burma, Thailand, Malaysia and Indonesia.

The peoples of the curry lands have honed and perfected the art of vegetarian cooking to the point where it cannot be improved upon. They use spices and other flavourings to add zest and enormous interest to the humblest ingredient. They make it great.

One thing is for certain: no one should be put off by the thought that this is a boring collection of recipes all of which are variations on cabbages and nuts. Nothing could be further from the truth. The choice of ingredients that the vegetarian has is eye-opening. I suppose we all think we know about vegetables, but I was astonished to find that there are over 80 different types of vegetables alone, including leaves, shoots, squashes (marrow types), bulbs, roots, tubers, pods and seeds. Add to this at least as many fruits, nuts, dried pulses, grains, flour, noodles and, for all but vegans, dairy products and eggs, and the list is enormous.

The first thing I like to do with a newly collected recipe is to test it for myself. If it turns out well I cook it for one of our Curry Club 'dinner nights', which may be for as many as 60 people at a time. Over a period of four years it has been possible to 'test' hundreds of recipes on members. In fact, nearly all the recipes in this book have been tested in this way. Together they provide a wonderful wealth of vegetarian delights bringing together complementary textures, colours and tastes.

Whether you are a vegetarian, a demi-vegetarian, a vegan or an interested meat eater wishing to extend your curry cooking range, I hope you will find, as I do, that you will be able to produce anything from a crispy snack to a five course meal as the mood takes you, without a piece of meat in sight. I am not a full convert myself yet, but who knows – with dishes like these who needs meat anyway?

Pat Chapman
The Curry Club

CHAPTER ONE

Culinary Background

Archaeological evidence has proved that India has been cooking with spices for at least 7,000 years. Indeed today's distinctly different northern Indian style using whole aromatic mild spices and the south's use of pungent, hot spices wet-ground with garlic and onion have changed remarkably little over the millennia. The spices of India became objects of trade and high value as early as 2000 BC, when traders from China and from Arabia developed sufficient navigational and marine skills to voyage to India, to bring their spices there as well as to take native Indian spices home with them. The people, too, began to migrate and lands such as Bangladesh and Burma became populated around the time of Christ.

The northwest land passage linked the Middle East to India via Iran, Afghanistan and Pakistan, and many invaders came from west to east.

It was the Moslems, who began to arrive in India from the eighth century, who left the most enduring cultural influences on India.

Certain curry lands such as Nepal in the north, high in the Himalayas, owe much of their cultural development to Budhism. So too did Thailand – a curry-loving nation to the east of Burma. Sri-Lanka is the pearl-shaped island to the south of India. All of these lands have distinctive indigenous populations who enjoy curry.

Population movements over the last few centuries have led to the establishment of Indian populations as far apart as Malaya, Singapore, Indonesia, East Africa and the West Indies. These communities were mostly moved there by the British as part of the mechanism of their empire. In the last few decades most English-speaking nations have encouraged the establishment of Asian communities of significant proportions, and it is this which has led to the appreciation of curry in Australasia, Canada, America and Britain.

One quarter of the world's population are curry eaters and many of these are vegetarian. It is hardly surprising that their delightful 'staple' has spread to other parts of the world.

Vegetarianism in India

Among the earliest inhabitants of India were, in the north, the dairy-farming Ayrans and, in the south, the rice-cultivating Dravidians.

The Aryans were meat eaters but, in the course of time, the numbers of cattle they bred for meat and milk became smaller in relation to the expanding population, and the cow eventually came to be revered, not slaughtered. By 1000 BC this dogma had become a definite characteristic of the Hindu religion. Meat eating gave way to vegetarianism, with a large dependence on dairy produce. The Dravidians, meanwhile, had evolved away from meat eating very early on, relying instead on their rice, coconut and prolific vegetable crops for subsistance.

Apart from the peoples living by the coast or near rivers, who ate fish, India remained almost totally vegetarian for the next 2,000 years.

At this time the races in the Middle East were herders of sheep and goats and breeders of poultry. The ancient Egyptians had developed incubators and hatcheries long before the birth of Christ. Following the birth of Mohammed in 570 AD, the population became Moslem, and soon they ruled a vast empire which included northern India.

The greatest empire which India ever saw was that of the Moghuls. From 1500 until they were finally replaced by the British in 1857, the Moghuls ruled the sub-continent of India in a style of extraordinary power and wealth. The early Moslems had brought their meat-eating culture into India and the Moghuls, who were also Moslems, consolidated this.

Most Moslems are meat eaters. Most Hindus are vegetarian. This makes a total of over 75 per cent of India's population, some 450 million people, vegetarians. Nowhere else on earth has such a large concentration of vegetarians, and nowhere else has more delicious vegetarian food.

Towards Vegetarianism in the West

It is only in the last couple of decades that the populations of the West have become highly diet-conscious. Recent research has shown a direct relationship between the consumption of meat, particularly fatty red meat, and heart disease. Consequently surveys are indicating that sales of red meat are declining whilst sales of white meat and fish are on the increase.

There are many other factors which contribute to long-term ill health including chemicals in processed foods and one's general state of fitness. But the consumer's awareness is now heightened to the pitfalls of the modern Western diet, and people are looking for solutions.

Vegetarianism is a partial solution, but its benefits can be wasted if one simply ceases to eat meat, poultry and fish, whilst continuing to eat fatty, cholesterol-laden dairy products and processed foods to excess. In any case, health is not the only reason for people choosing to stop eating meat. Financial, sentimental, allergic and/or ethical reasons may be contributory motivators, or simply the fact that the individual was brought up as a vegetarian.

The fact remains that, even with the new trends away from meat eating, the vast majority of the Western populations are not vegetarians – in Britain, around 95 per cent eat meat. With that in mind, the contents of this book are all the more interesting. Most of us will probably only ever be part-time vegetarians, but we can all benefit from a healthier diet.

The Modern Vegetarian

We immediately think of a vegetarian as someone who, quite simply, does not eat meat. However, nothing in life is simple and vegetarian definitions are no exception.

In fact there are a number of vegetarian subdivisions, some of which are not at all obvious. These are the definitions as supplied by The Vegetarian Society (see below).

Vegetarians
Persons who eat no meat, fowl or fish, nor do they consume any by-products of the slaughterhouse (such as gelatine).

Vegans
The same as vegetarians; in addition they do not eat dairy products and eggs. Strict vegans will not eat honey either.

True Vegetarians
Same definitions as vegans, although some vegans dislike this term.

Strict Vegetarians
Same as true vegetarians.

Lacto Vegetarians
As vegetarians; will eat dairy products but not eggs.

Ovo Vegetarians
As vegetarians; will eat eggs but not dairy products.

Lacto-Ovo Vegetarians
Will eat dairy products and eggs, i.e. this is a precise definition of vegetarians.

For more information on the above and about vegetarianism in general, please contact The Vegetarian Society, Parkdale, Dunham Road, Altringham, Cheshire, WA14 4QG.

Recipes marked with the following symbol are suitable for vegans: ☑

HEALTHY EATING

Curry owes a great many of its delicious tastes and textures to the use of spices and of fat. This is good news and bad for the strictly health-conscious diner. Good news because spices have medicinal attributes when used in these relatively small amounts – some aid digestion, whilst some fight bacteria or help to kill pain. We are all familiar with the use of clove solution in dentistry. The bad news concerns the use of fat in Indian cookery. Very nearly every Indian dish uses fat of some kind. You simply cannot establish a correctly textured base without it.

I like to use sufficient fat to ensure that the spices and other ingredients are well cooked. However, there is no need for any dish to be served swimming in it, as seems to be the practice at certain restaurants. It is unnecessary, unhealthy, does not contribute to the quality of the dish and should have been spooned off before serving.

The debate about which is the healthiest fat to use wages back and forth. Solid fats (lard, dripping, ghee, butter and hard margarine) are high in saturated fats and cholesterol, whilst certain non-congealing oils such as sunflower and soya oil are referred to as polyunsaturates. Recent research has indicated that it is mono–unsaturated oils that are the healthiest to use for cooking and these include olive, peanut and mustard oils. Olive oil has too dominant a flavour to be used in curry cooking, but peanut (also called groundnut) oil and mustard oil are good. The latter is widely used in southern India, whilst ghee is the standard cooking fat in the north.

I have tried every type of oil available over the years and, in my view, it makes no difference to the taste of a curry that is cooked for any length of time which oil is used. So if in doubt avoid solid fats. The recipes to which this maxim does not apply are those such as rice and breads where the taste of the ghee really counts.

Carbohydrates and fibre (roughage) are available in plenty from the curry lands' staples – wheat and rice. Lentils are as rich in protein as meat, and vegetables supply minerals and vitamins. Many curry restaurants tend to overcook their vegetables, destroying vitamin C, but at home you can control this and cook vegetables minimally to a crisp texture, thus retaining more goodness. The few excuses to eat raw vegetables in the Indian regime include salad garnishes and fresh chutneys. Fresh onion is said to be immensely good for one, and it happens to accompany Indian food admirably. Finally, dairy products are important ingredients in India, especially in the north. From a dietary point of view their benefit is calcium.

Taken as a whole, Indian cuisine supplies everything needed for a balanced diet.

The following table is reproduced with the permission of the Vegetarian Society (see page 11). It shows the essential nutrients supplied by animal products, that could be lacking in a vegetarian diet, and gives the main alternative sources.

nutrient	principal sources	advice
Protein	Soya protein, nuts, pulses, grains, milk, cheese, free range eggs and potatoes.	Mix the proteins you eat to get a good balance.
Iron	Baked beans, wholemeal bread, dried fruit, cocoa, pulses, millet, nuts, molasses, leafy green vegetables, brewers and bakers yeast.	A higher proportion of iron is absorbed if taken with vitamin C, so eat plenty of salads and fresh fruit. Women need more iron than men to replace that lost during menstruation.
Calcium	Soya milk, milk, cheese, free range eggs, leafy green veg, wholemeal bread, sesame seeds and tahini, potatoes and also fortified flours.	Growing children and nursing mothers require more than the normal daily amounts, so supplement your usual intake. Vitamin D helps to absorb more calcium and is formed mainly by exposure to sun/day light.
Vitamin B12	Many soya proteins are fortified, yeast extract, some soya milks are fortified, also milk, cheese and free range eggs.	Vegetarians who use milk, cheese or eggs have no need to worry. It is recommended that vegans have 1 cup of soya milk daily.

All other vitamins, minerals and other nutrients are found in plentiful supply in a well-balanced vegetarian diet.

Here is a checklist of foods that should be eaten every day to ensure that your diet is complete. Try to include something from each group if possible but don't worry if you miss one or two out now and then!

1. Pulses, nuts and seeds – beans, lentils, sesame seeds, almonds, hazels, etc.
2. Cereals – wheat (in wholemeal bread), rice, oats, millet, couscous, rye, etc.
3. Dried fruits – apricots, peaches are especially high in iron.
4. Fresh fruits.
5. Salads and vegetables – especially dark green leafy veg like watercress, broccoli, cabbage and orange vegetables like carrots and tomatoes.
6. Soya products – soya protein, tofu, soya flour, soya milk (excellent, fat-free source of protein).
7. Oils and vegetable fats.
8. Potatoes – to alternate with cereals.
9. Yeast extracts – essential for vitamin B12 for vegans.

KITCHEN EQUIPMENT

I have made the point in previous books that the kitchen belonging to the villager in the third world is a primitive affair. It is very bare, usually devoid of furniture. The work is done in the lotus position on the floor. It will not be blessed with running water, electricity or gas. Water is collected from the village well or stream and is lugged back home in narrow-necked, wide-bellied earthenware vessels, in a tedious round trip which may be short or may be miles. The same journey will be made two or even three times each day.

Cooking is carried out over charcoal, wood or dry dung-cake fires. Elbow grease is the prime motive power. An array of tools and cooking pots hang on hooks on the walls, and a variety of spice-grinding stones are kept on a shelf.

It is of interest to note the way they do things in village India to great effect. In good weather (i.e. outside of the monsoon and winter) a lot of cooking is done out of doors. Sometimes shallow pits are dug and charcoal or wood fires lit in them. The earthenware or metal cooking vessel is placed on the fire and surrounded by coals. Even the lid is covered with burning embers and the whole dish is left to simmer for hours. The thrifty Indian villagers learned a long time ago to use all available resources – and fuel is no exception. The sacred cow stars in this story – its dung is collected and compressed into flat round cakes, then dried rock hard in the sun. These are then stacked in 'stooks', resembling large beehives. The cakes burn efficiently and I'm assured that they are odour-free.

In all the curry lands the kitchen is the women's domain. It is kept scrupulously clean. Shoes are removed and hands are washed before it is entered. And out of the simplest kitchen often come the most exquisite meals. I know, because I have been in a good few.

It's a far cry from our electrified, gadget-packed, fitted kitchen, complete with hot and cold running water, oven, stove, microwave, refrigerator, freezer and stainless-steel double sink unit. The Indian villager would regard what we take completely for granted with more amazement than we would if we were beamed up to the flight deck of the Star Ship Enterprise.

However, I am not suggesting that we send all our gadgets to the jumble sale, cut off the water, electricity and gas and bring in the dung cakes in order to reproduce the authentic village masterpiece. We can achieve equally good results on a normal gas or electric stove, ceramic or Aga or, for that matter, a camping stove. Although not to be found in the traditional Indian kitchen nor much used in the restaurant, I find that the oven is a highly effective way of cooking curries. The all-round heat finishes the cooking of the spices and produces a curry of excellent taste and texture, needing little attention and without the tedium and 'burn-risk' factor that cooking on the stove is prone to. This technique would be impossible for a village Indian (hence it is never mentioned in 'authentic' cookbooks). Yet it is not dissimilar to the slow-cooking technique mentioned earlier.

My objective in this book is to produce the tastiest dishes in the least onerous way. Not for me the chore of grinding or chopping by hand if a machine will do it. Nor do I relish standing stirring at the stove when a casserole dish in the oven requires no effort. Why do a repetitive job 10 times when a big effort once and the freezer reduce the task to a single cooking and washing up session? I am not advocating a lazy cooking style, however – there is plenty of work to be done to achieve excellence in these recipes. I am simply saying that I endeavour to use methods which save work rather than to create work for work's sake.

Your kitchen should possess the following items to cook the recipes in this book:

- knives
- chopping board
- mixing bowls: large, medium, small
- *karahi** or wok or large frying pan
- *tava*** or griddle pan or large frying pan
- casserole dish(es): 5 pint (3 litre)
- saucepans with lids: 5 pint (3 litre), 4 pint (2.25 litre), $2\frac{1}{4}$ pint (1.3 litre)
- oven tray(s)
- grill tray with wire rack

* the *karahi* is the Indian equivalent of the wok
** the *tava* is a flat griddle pan
   See glossary for further details.

ELECTRICAL TOOLS

It is with these tools that we can save time.

Blender
The device for making soups and purées requiring some liquid but which achieves the correct texture for curries.

Food Processor
An expensive but immensely useful kitchen tool. Its standard blade can be used to make purées, although even with added water they are not of as fine a texture as those made in a blender. Other blades include vegetable shredders and slicers.

Coffee Grinder
An effective way to grind spices. It can handle most spices and grind them reasonably finely. Best results are obtained when the spices are 'roasted' (see page 24) and cooled first and the machine is not loaded past the half way mark. A damp wipe leaves the machine ready to handle coffee beans without tainting them.

Spice Mill
A new attachment for 'Chef' units which grinds all spices, raw or roasted, to any degree of fineness you want.

Dough Hook Attachment
A great time and effort saver.

Rice Cooker

In my view, a total extravagance. But if you want one or have one, then use it and you'll get good results.

Warming Drawer

In the chapters on rice and bread I mention the use of a warming drawer. Some ovens have these, but if yours doesn't, use the oven itself on its lowest setting.

Microwave

A much maligned kitchen tool, the microwave seems to be regarded by some as the enemy of real cooking. I've heard people say that 'real' restaurants or cooks would not use a microwave. This is rubbish, of course. It gets its poor reputation as the purveyor of soggy pub pies, a role in which it performs at its worst. The microwave is a high-speed cooker with limitations.

Like the food processor, it is invaluable in some roles and useless in others. It is great for fast thawing of frozen foods, for casseroling and for reheating wet dishes. It boils water fast and is excellent for blanching vegetables, and it cooks papadoms. But in my experience, it does not handle the initial frying (bargar) of spices and purées effectively, and it is hopeless for cooking or reheating pastry.

Microwaves vary in power from 350 watts to 2000 watts (the latter being ultra-powerful, very fast catering units), the average being 650 watts. Cooking times depend on the power of your particular machine, so again your own experience is your best guide. I'm not absolutely sold on the theory that microwaving detracts from flavours. There seems to be no scientific reason for it.

Pressure Cookers

These will indeed cook many things very fast. But I'm old fashioned and find they make things mushy and rather tasteless. I thought I'd found the perfect use for my pressure cooker when cooking lentils, which it does 150 per cent faster than the conventional method, until a lentil got stuck in the relief valve one time. It was lucky that I noticed it early on, when the hissy jingling stopped. Even so, it had built up a dangerous pressure, and I've heard stories of exploding cookers. So I went off the whole idea. New pressure cookers, however, should be fine.

COOKING METHODS FOR VEGETABLES

Until well into this century, vegetables were regarded with considerable dislike. This was probably due to the cooking method.

They were invariably overcooked – not by the odd minute or two, but by hours. I have in my Granny's old cookery book, dated 1898, a number of vegetable recipes. To cook carrots, it states (and I quote verbatim), 'put them in boiling water with some salt, and boil them from two to three hours. Very young carrots will require one hour.' I don't need to test that recipe to picture the results. Little wonder vegetables were detested.

The concept of minimal cooking to retain the crunch and goodness of vegetables is relatively new. I should make the point that this is the way I prefer my vegetables so you'll find that my cooking times in the recipes that follow are very brief. If you prefer a softer texture, cook for longer until you have it as you like it.

These are the three stove-top cooking techniques for vegetables.

Boiling

Bring an ample quantity of water to the boil. Add the prepared raw vegetables and simmer until you have the texture you require. Keep the liquid for subsequent stock.

Steaming

This technique retains the most flavour. Water is boiled in the steamer base. The vegetables are placed on the steamer tray which fits snugly above and clear of the boiling water. Put the lid on and steam until you get the texture you require. It is well worth buying a steamer if you don't already have one.

Stir-frying

Some vegetables can be cooked from raw without water, by stir-frying in oil. Best results are obtained by using flat thin items (such as mangetout and green beans) or by cutting thin strips or slices. Do not have the heat too high. Medium heat will cook the vegetables in a few minutes without burning them as long as you keep stirring them.

Other techniques include baking, casseroling, microwaving and pressure cooking. In some of the following recipes I have used the former two techniques, and have discussed the general principles of the latter two on page 16.

SOME USEFUL TIPS

As I potter about my kitchen or talk to other chefs, I frequently stumble across small but highly useful tips and mini-techniques which all add up to better cooking. Here is a pot-pourri of unrelated items which will, I hope, be helpful for all your cooking, not just for 'currying'.

Batter
To make batter crisper, use very little or no water – use instead yoghurt, lemon juice, etc. Also half-fry the items, rest them for 10 minutes (or more), then finish off, serving at once for crispest results. Try this in the recipe on page 116.

Bean sprouts
These are made by allowing green moong dhal and other lentils to germinate, which requires water and the correct temperature. To sprout dry lentils, soak them overnight, rinse in warm water, strain then spread them out on kitchen paper. Put them in a dark, warm place for 24 hours. Inspect, rinse in warm water, strain and leave on kitchen paper in a dark warm place. Repeat the process until they sprout, then leave in a light place until about an inch in length.

Bombay mix
If this goes soft because it has been stored without a lid, place it in the oven at 225°F/180°C/Gas $\frac{1}{4}$ for 10 minutes or so. When it cools it will be really crisp. This technique also applies to cereals, biscuits, etc.

Breadcrumbing
In place of conventional breadcrumbs use semolina (which is made from hard wheat or durum flour). This can also be used to flour an item for frying. It does not go so 'soggy', thus the result is crisper.

Capsicum peppers
To obtain nice shapes from capsicums or sweet peppers – diamonds, squares or julienne strips (matchsticks) – cut off the top and bottom. Slit down one side and open out to a rectangle. Cut away the pithy centre and shake off the seeds. Cut to the required shapes.

Chickpeas/hard beans
These items need an overnight soak and a lengthy boil to bring to readiness (page 66). I find it easiest to do this to a whole bag (usually 500 g). Freeze the surplus and use like frozen peas.

Cleansing hands
Onion, garlic and greasy curry smells can linger on the hands, no matter how many times you wash them, it seems. Try 'washing' your hands with a quarter

of a lemon (used like a scrubbing brush). It degreases them effectively. Then wash with soap and water.

Coriander, fresh leaves

These are used a lot in Indian and other 'ethnic' cooking styles. The leaves are easily grown and are readily available in wholesale vegetable markets. Yet many high street green grocers do not stock coriander. You need to find the ones that do, and the answer is to do a bit of detective work. Find out which greengrocer(s) in your area supplies the Indian restaurants. Then, hey presto, you've found your fresh coriander supplier.

Another point about coriander leaves is that they quickly go soggy if they get wet. So when you clean them use minimal water, then pat dry.

Curry texture

If a curry goes too dry during cooking (or more particularly when reheating from cold or after freezing), the addition of water alone may lose the good texture the curry had to start with. Instead add water *and* oil in the ratio 2 parts water:1 part vegetable oil.

Egg sizes

There are seven EC grades: Grade 1 is 70 g ($2\frac{1}{2}$ oz) or over; Grade 4 is 55–60 g (2 oz); Grade 7 is 45 g ($1\frac{1}{2}$ oz) or under.

Egg timings

To hard-boil a Grade 1 egg, immerse it in boiling water. Remove after exactly 15 minutes and cool at once in cold water. Longer cooking results in a blue ring around the yolk. A quail egg takes 4 minutes to hard-boil.

To prevent an egg cracking when boiling, do not waste salt, oil or vinegar in the water. Simply prick the blunt end of the egg with a pin, piercing only just through the shell. This allows the air in the air sac to escape as it expands when immersed in boiling water.

Fermentation

Certain foods have a tendency to ferment. Lentils, especially, will do so if the temperature is above a certain minimum. This is what we want to happen with yeast in flour to make dough rise (page 140), but we don't want it to happen unexpectedly. It can happen with vegetable and lentil combinations (dhansak, for example). The initial signs are a sour, bitter taste and smell, and slight bubbling when cold. In an advanced state the dish will literally start rising; the texture becomes purée-like and it smells bad. It can only be thrown away. Fermentation can be prevented by serving the dish within a reasonable time after cooking, or by cooling in a refrigerator or freezing.

Garlic
If garlic burns during the initial stages of cooking you must throw it away, or else it will retain a bitter taste throughout. Indeed my maxim, 'if it burns, bin it', applies to all cooking at early stages.

Gram flour (besan)
This must be stored in an airtight container. It can turn sour after a few months, so buy little and often.

Ice-cube mould
Keep one of these available for freezing small quantities of purée: garlic, ginger, coriander, etc. Use yoghurt pots for moulding larger quantities of chopped or puréed onion, curry purées, etc. Once frozen, ease the items out of the moulds and keep them in labelled freezer bags.

Saffron
An excellent way to extract saffron colour without losing its flavour is to place strands in rose or kewra (screwpine) water and leave them for a few days. By then the water will have become a deep orange-gold colour and you can sprinkle a few drops of it on the dishes of your choice. It will keep indefinitely.

Smells
Yes, curry making is smelly! In particular, the initial cooking of garlic and onion (it's no worse than French cooking!) plus some spices, makes smells which linger. You can do much of this background work in advance in bulk (this also saves on washing up), and use your freezer. To minimise smells, here are some tips. Firstly, close the kitchen door and open windows whilst cooking. Run your extractor fan if you have one.

After cooking you can create further, more acceptable smells. Estate agents' tricks are interesting. They advise that a house smelling of freshly roasted coffee and/or bread, or fresh flowers and a newly mown lawn (difficult under several feet of snow) is more likely to attract a buyer than one smelling of curry. Personally, I can't see what's wrong with the smell of curry, but two further smell over-riders are vanilla pods lightly baked in the oven and joss sticks.

Sugar
If a dish tastes a little too sour for your taste, add any sugar, $\frac{1}{2}$ teaspoon at a time, stirring and tasting until you are happy. Fructose is the natural sugar from fruit and a new granulated fructose sugar is available at a fraction of the calorific 'value' of ordinary white sugar (sucrose).

Tomato
Only add tomato to a dish towards the end of cooking. It can cause the dish to become bitter if put in too early.

PORTIONS

Most of the recipes in this book serve four people (except where stated) with average appetites. I normally allow $1\frac{1}{2}$ lb (675 g) nett of the principal ingredients of a main course i.e. after it is shorn of peel husks, stalks – anything inedible – for four servings. Usually there is about $\frac{1}{2}$ lb (225 g) of extra items in a dish, to give about 8 oz (225 g) per person in total.

For an accompanying main course dish allow 3 oz (75 g) per person; for rice allow 2–3 oz (50–75 g) uncooked weight; for dried lentils, 1 oz (25 g).

These quantities are given for guidance only. Appetites vary enormously. One person may eat two or even three times as much as another. Also, the composition of an Indian meal could be one main dish with rice, or a number of main dishes with rice and bread. So, as with all aspects of cooking, common sense should prevail.

If you wish to cook for one person, either scale down the quantities or use the freezer. If you wish to cook for more than four, scale up. Taste and adjust as you go – if you feel a particular dish needs more spices – add some. Flexibility is, as always, the key.

FOR THE CURRY PARTY

There can hardly be a better style of food for the dinner party or the large buffet-style event, providing you know that all your guests enjoy curry. It is tasty, varied, colourful and different – with lots for your guests and yourself to talk about. Yet even the most complicated array of dishes can largely be prepared well in advance of your guests' arrival.

Bases for vegetable curries can be prepared in advance and the vegetables themselves can be blanched, then cooled in cold water, on the morning of the event. Papadoms and rice can be cooked in the afternoon and kept warm until required – even bread dough can be on standby. With careful planning, all you should need to do 'on the night' is to finish off any stir-fry dishes, reheat pre-cooked dishes in your oven and roll out and cook your breads.

When entertaining, avoid stretching yourself too far. Do not attempt a recipe which requires a technique you have never tried before, and do not cook a meal which requires more cooking rings or space than you have available.

ALCOHOL AND BEVERAGES

Curry has a peculiar reputation when it comes to drink. One school of opinion states that no Indian drinks alcohol, for religious reasons. Another states that the only alcoholic beverage which goes with curry is lager and that wines are wasted. Neither is correct. Most Indians are Hindus and they have no laws regarding alcoholic consumption. It is the Moslems who are not permitted to drink alcohol. As for lager, if you like it then you'll enjoy it with curry. The same can be said, in my view, about wine, despite warnings from many critics that wine is wasted on spicy food.

The facts are simple: wine, red or white, is perfectly acceptable with curry. The more delicately spiced the dish, the more sophisticated can be the wine. More than one top-class Indian restaurant offers premier crux Bordeaux on its wine list. But such a wine would be wasted if your palate craved a searingly hot or pungently spiced dish. The choice, as they say, is yours. Wining and dining is for enjoyment – rules are for fools. My personal favourite with curry is pink champagne or sparkling wine – it makes a nice talking point at a party.

There is a flourishing alcohol industry in India. Lager-style beers are brewed and bottled all over the country, and in certain areas wines are produced. The best of these is indisputably the 'champagne' produced in the Bombay area under French consultancy and marketed as 'Omar Khayam'. Although it cannot technically be called champagne, because it is not grown in the champagne area, the result is indistinguishable. The Indian white wine Veena is lightly spiced and makes a pleasant change, but their red wines and many other whites are rather heavy and resinous. Indian spirits – whisky, gin, brandy and vodka – are equally rough but they are relatively cheap.

All of these alcoholic processes were introduced to India by her European conquerors, notably the Portuguese and the British, so they have only been established in the country in relatively recent times (in the last few centuries). It is not surprising, therefore, that the habit of drinking alcohol has not overtaken a population whose civilisation began thousands of years ago. To this day, although the middle and wealthy classes enjoy the odd tipple (and the best present you can take an Indian host is a bottle of Johnny Walker 'Black Label' Scotch whisky – the price in India is six times what it is in Scotland) most people enjoy fruit juice and yoghurt drinks.

CHAPTER TWO

Curry Bases and Basics

The entire contents of this chapter have been reprinted from my previous curry book, *The Curry Club Favourite Restaurant Curries*. The information is fundamental to the successful cooking of all the subsequent newly published recipes in this book. Its importance cannot be underestimated; it takes the reader step by step through all the vital techniques required to convert raw spices and ingredients into correctly prepared blends, purées and flavourings.

STORING SPICES

Whole spices retain their flavour longer than ground, for one year or more sometimes. Ground spices give off a stronger aroma than whole, and of course this means their storage life is that much shorter. Three months is about right for most ground items. So plan your larder accordingly, and buy little and often and grind freshly. Keep the spices out of sunlight (better in a dark pantry) and in airtight labelled containers. Coffee or jam jars are excellent.

GRINDING SPICES

It is better by far to grind your own whole spices whenever you can. Firstly you can be sure of the quality and contents, and secondly they will be fresher and tastier. The traditional method is by mortar and pestle, but you can use an electric coffee grinder or the new Kenwood spice mill. After a damp wipe a coffee grinder can still be used for coffee – it might even enhance the flavour! Use small quantities to prevent overloading the motor.

Don't try to grind dry ginger or turmeric. They are too fibrous for most small grinders, and commercial powders are adequate. Peppers – chilli, paprika and black or white pepper – are tricky, and commercially ground powders will suffice. The oilier spices such as cloves, nutmeg, brown cardamoms and bay leaves are easier to grind if roasted first.

In the recipes, when a spice if referred to as 'ground', this means factory ground. Where it requires the spice to be home ground (usually after roasting), the recipe clearly states this.

ROASTING SPICES

Whole spices are roasted to enhance or change the flavour. The process is simple and can be done in a dry pan on the stove, in a dry electric frying pan, under the grill or in the oven. Each spice should be heated until it gives off an aroma. The heat should be medium rather than hot and the time required is a few minutes. The spice should not blacken, a light brown at most is sufficient. The original oil of the spice must not be totally cooked out or it will lose its flavour. A little experimenting will soon show you how to do it. In some recipes pre-roasted spices are important (see pages 80 and 119).

CURRY TECHNIQUES

There are several ways of utilising the spices and flavourings for curry making, and it is necessary to outline these before we begin.

The first 'stage' is the mixing together of the ground spices, the masala – the unique combination which makes Indian style cooking so distinctive. The following curry powder recipe is a masala, but throughout the recipes I refer to the masala as **spices** (whole or ground).

As the spices need to be cooked slightly to get rid of raw tastes, the next step is to make them into a paste with a little water. The cooking can be done by simply adding the powder to hot oil (many restaurant cooks do this), but it is very easy to burn the spices this way, and a paste is safer. The cooking of the masala – the bhoona – is the next stage.

The cooking of whole spices as opposed to ground – the bargar – is another technique which I outline, as is the puréeing and cooking of onion, ginger and garlic.

Mild Curry Powder

Commercial curry powder has two drawbacks in my view. Firstly, although the manufacturers are supposed to list the ingredients, some avoid it by simply stating 'spices'; and even if they do list them, they do not state the quantities. They often put in too much chilli, salt and, in some cases, chemical colourings and preservatives. Undeclared additives can include husks and stalks and other adulterations.

The second drawback is that the use of the same curry powder blend in all the recipes would make each dish taste virtually the same.

However, it is sometimes useful to have curry powder in the larder. You can purchase a commercial version or you can make up your own with this interesting mixture. It comes from the first cookery book given to a young bride who, with her husband, was posted to the British army base in Agra in 1904. The lady was my grandmother and that book was her bible. It was first published in 1870, so this curry powder has been recipe tested for 120 years, in itself an amazing fact.

The following recipe will give you about 9 oz (250 g) of curry powder.

A heaped teaspoon is about 5 g on average. It's not easy to transpose to Imperial.

60 g coriander seeds	20 g aromatic garam masala
30 g white cummin seeds	5 g dry ground curry leaves
20 g fenugreek seeds	5 g asafoetida
25 g gram flour (besan)	5 g ginger powder
25 g garlic powder	5g chilli powder
20 g paprika	5 g yellow mustard powder
20 g turmeric	5 g ground black pepper

1 Roast and then grind the first three spices.

2 Mix all together well and store.

3 Omit the final four spices for a totally mild curry powder.

4 For those who wish, salt and sugar (white granulated) can be added during the blending: add 2 tablespoons sugar and/or 1 teaspoon salt.

To make a dish for four you would need about 1 oz (25 g) of curry powder, so this will give you enough for 10 curries. I prefer to make a reasonable batch like 9 oz (250 g) because it 'matures' or becomes better blended the longer it is stored. It can be used at once, of course, but after about a month it is perfect. Do not keep it for longer than 18 months – it tends to lose its subtle flavours, becoming bitter. Store in an airtight container in a dark damp-free place.

The Masala Paste

When a recipe states 'mix and blend dry spices' (a masala), as in the previous curry powder mixture, it is necessary to cook those spices to remove the raw tastes. This is most safely done by making up a paste with water to obtain a thickish texture. The water prevents the spices from burning up when they are introduced to the oil in the bhoona or frying process.

1 Select a mixing bowl large enough to enable you to stir the masala.

2 Stir the masala until it is fully mixed.

3 Add enough water to form a stiff paste *and no more*.

4 Leave to stand for a minimum of 10 minutes. It does not matter how *long* it stands. This ensures that the ground spices absorb all the water.

5 Add a little water if it is too dry prior to using in the bhoona or frying process.

The Bhoona

The bhoona is the Hindi term for the process of cooking the spice paste in hot oil. This is an important part of the curry cooking process which removes the raw taste of the spices and influences the final taste of the dish. Use the bhoona method whenever the recipes in this book state that you should 'fry the spices'. In fact, traditionally you should fry the spice paste first, then add the puréed or chopped onion second. This method can easily cause burned spices so I reverse the process and have found that it works very satisfactorily.

1 Take a round-sided pan such as a *karahi* or wok. If you don't have one, use an ordinary frying pan (a non-stick one is best).

2 Heat the oil to quite a high heat (but not smoking).

3 Remove the pan from the heat and at once gently add the onion purée. Return to the heat and commence stirring.

4 *From this point do not let your attention wander.* Keep stirring the purée until the oil is hot again, then gently add the masala paste. Beware of splattering.

5 Keep stirring. The water in the paste lowers the temperature. Do not let the mixture stick at all. Do not stop stirring, not even for a few seconds.

6 After a few minutes the water will have evaporated out and the oil will float above the mixture. The spices will be cooked. Remove the pan from the heat. Proceed with the remainder of the recipe.

The Bargar

Some of the recipes in this book require you to fry *whole* spices. The process is for the same reason as the bhoona – to cook out the raw taste from the spices. Again the oil should be hot, and the spices are put into the oil with no water or purée. You must use your judgement as to when they are cooked. Do not let them blacken. As soon as they begin to change colour or to float they are ready. It will not take more than a couple of minutes.

If you do burn the spices during the bhoona or bargar process *you must throw the result away and start again.* Better to waste a small amount of spices than taint a whole meal.

THE PURÉE

The importance of the purée cannot be overstated, and it is the way that restaurants achieve that gorgeous creamy texture. It is based on tradition, of course. In the Indian home the purée is made the hard way by wet-grinding spices with garlic and/or ginger and/or onion to a fine texture, and it is time-consuming and messy. We are fortunate to have electric blenders and food processors to do the job in seconds. I have heard a purist school of thought which says that metal blades taint the items being ground, but every restaurant uses this method and it doesn't seem to taint their dishes.

I have given large quantities for each of these purées as it saves time, smells and washing up to make large batches and freeze the surplus in ice-cube moulds or empty yoghurt tubs.

Garlic Purée

Real garlic is best. I still use garlic powder from time to time but it contains flour and gives a distinctive flavour. An expensive (but good) product is garlic purée in tubes. A product I have used a lot recently (as do many restaurants) is dehydrated garlic flakes: to use, soak in an equal volume of water for 30 minutes then mulch down in a food processor or blender. The taste is nearly as good as the real (fresh) thing, and the texture is indistinguishable.

One plump clove of garlic is the equivalent of 1 level teaspoon garlic purée. An ice-cube container holds 3 teaspoons of purée.

30 plump garlic cloves, peeled

1 Mulch the garlic cloves around in a blender or food processor, adding no water or a minimum amount.

2 Scrape the garlic purée out of the container, place in 10 ice-cube moulds and freeze raw.

Ginger Purée

In my first book I stated that ginger had to be peeled before using. This is the way it has always been done. The skin of the ginger root causes a bitter taste, so it is said. But shortly after that first book was published I started to experiment and found that if ginger is mulched down it does not cause bitterness if the skin is left on. Remove the really rough ends or dirty bits, but leave any nice pink skin. This saves a great deal of time.

If you use dehydrated ginger, it must be soaked for several hours otherwise it is too hard.

1 lb (450 g) fresh ginger, trimmed of
hard knobs but unpeeled

1 Coarsely chop the ginger, then mulch it down in a blender or food processor.

2 Scrape out of the container, place in 10 ice-cube moulds and freeze raw.

Onion Purée

Onions do not freeze whole at all well. As they are very watery they become soggy when they thaw, which is fine for boiling and subsequent puréeing but no use if you want to chop and fry them. Raw chopped and puréed onion freezes and thaws satisfactorily.

Unlike garlic and ginger, I find that onion needs to be boiled (blanched) in hot water first before puréeing, otherwise it has a very bitter taste.

10 Spanish onions, about 8 oz (225 g)
each, peeled

1 Coarsely chop the onions and place them in boiling water. Strain after 3 minutes.

2 Mulch down in a blender or food processor until very fine in texture.

3 Scrape out of the container, place in 10 yoghurt pots and freeze.

Tamarind Purée

Tamarind (*imli*) – also known as the Indian date – is a major souring agent, particularly in southern Indian cooking. The tamarind tree bears pods of about 6–8 inches (15–20 cm) long which become dark brown when ripe. These pods contain seeds and pulp, which are preserved indefinitely for use in cooking by compression into a rectangular block weighing about 11 oz (300 g).

To use the tamarind block, soak it overnight in twice its volume of hot water – about 23 fl oz (650 ml) per 11 oz (300 g) block. The next day pulp it well with your fingers, then strain through a sieve, discarding the husks. The brown liquid should be quite thick, and there will be plenty of it. Freeze any spare.

CURRY PASTES AND GRAVY

Anyone interested in Indian food must have encountered bottled curry pastes on the grocery shelves. There are many makes and types, but little explanation as to what they are or what they do. They are designed to take the labour out of blending a spice mixture, making it into a water paste and frying it. The manufacturers do it all for you, adding vinegar (acetic acid) and hot oil to prevent it from going mouldy. Unfortunately they also add salt and chilli powder which makes the pastes a little overpowering. They are very concentrated, and you only need a small quantity for cooking.

Curry pastes are already cooked, but to 'disguise' them you will probably need to add some other whole or ground spices, and you will certainly need to fry garlic, ginger, onion, etc. Simply add the spice paste after these three are fried and carry on with the rest of the recipe.

Home-made Bottled Curry Paste

The recipe below is for a mild paste which can form the base for many curry dishes. The quantities here will make a reasonable amount. Using vinegar (rather than all water) to make the paste will enable you to preserve it in jars. As with all pickling, sterilise the jars (a good hot wash in the dish washer followed by a dry out in a low-heat oven will do). Top off the paste in the jar with hot oil and inspect after a few days to see that there is no mould.

*250 g (1 recipe) mild curry powder
  (page 25)*
6–8 fl oz (175–250 ml) any vinegar
6–8 fl oz (175–250 ml) vegetable oil

1 Mix together the curry powder spices.

2 Add the vinegar and enough water to make a creamy paste.

3 Heat the oil in a *karahi* or wok.

4 Add the paste to the oil. It will splatter a bit so be careful.

5 Stir-fry the paste continually to prevent it sticking until the water content is cooked out (it should take about 5 minutes). As the liquid is reduced, the paste will begin to make a regular bubbling noise (hard to describe, but it goes chup-chup-chup-chup) if you don't stir, and it will splatter. This is your audible cue that it is ready. You can tell if the spices are cooked by taking the *karahi* off the stove. Leave to stand for 3–4 minutes. If the oil 'floats' to the top, the spices are cooked. If not, add a little more oil and repeat step 5.

6 Bottle the paste in sterilised jars.

7 Heat up a little more oil and 'cap' off the paste by pouring in enough oil to cover the paste. Seal the jars and store.

Curry Masala Gravy

Every curry restaurant has a large saucepan on the stove. In it is a pale orangey-gold gravy, quite thick in texture like apple purée. Taste and it's quite nice – a bit like a soup – or mild curry. Ask how it's made and like as not you'll get a shake of the head and a murmur about secrets of the trade. For this stock pot is one of the keys to achieving the restaurant curry. Recipes vary only slightly from chef to chef and restaurant to restaurant.

You can substitute this curry gravy for the individual garlic, ginger or onion purées given in many of the recipes which follow. Remember, this is just a mild base to which you can add other spices as required.

MAKES: enough stock for 10 curries (40 portions)

½ pint (300 ml) ghee or vegetable oil
5 tablespoons garlic purée (page 27)
4 tablespoons ginger purée (page 28)
1 full recipe onion purée (page 28)
6 tablespoons tomato purée
1 teaspoon salt

Spices
2 tablespoons turmeric
4 tablespoons curry powder (page 25)
1–6 teaspoons chilli powder (to taste)
2 tablespoons ground cummin seeds
2 tablespoons finely chopped fresh
    coriander leaves

1 Mix the **spices** with water to make a paste that has the approximate consistency of tomato ketchup. Let it stand whilst going to stage 2.

2 Heat the oil. Stir-fry the garlic purée for 3 minutes, then add the ginger purée and cook for 3 more minutes. Add the spice paste and stir-fry until the water has evaporated and the oil separates (about 5 minutes). Should it need it, add sufficient water to make the gravy pourable.

3 Add the onion purée and stir-fry for a further 10 minutes. Then add the tomato purée and stir-fry for a final 10 minutes. Add the salt.

4 Pour into 10 moulds and freeze.

Akhni Stock

Some restaurants make a strained stock as well as or in place of the previous curry masala gravy. This flavoured clear liquid, sometimes called yakhni, is used exactly like any vegetable stock at any time the recipe directs 'add water'. You can keep it in the fridge for a couple of days, but it is essential to re-boil it after this time; it will be safe for several re-boils, but use it finally in a soup or other cooking. Add the brine or water from tinned vegetables to your stock. You can top it up with fresh or leftover ingredients as required.

MAKES: 1½ pints (900 ml)

3 pints (1·75 litres) water
2 Spanish onions, peeled and chopped
1 teaspoon garlic purée (page 27)
1 teaspoon ginger purée (page 28)
1 tablespoon ghee
2 teaspoons salt

Spices (whole)
10 cloves
10 green cardamoms
6 pieces cassia bark
6 bay leaves

1 Boil the water, then add everything else.

2 Simmer for 1 hour with the lid on, by which time the stock should have reduced by half.

3 Strain and discard the solids.

Tandoori Dry Mix Masala

As with all pre-mixed masalas, this has the advantage of maturing during storage. Keep it in the dark in an airtight container, and it will be good for about 12 months.

45 g (3½ tablespoons) ground coriander
45 g (3½ tablespoons) ground cummin
45 g (3½ tablespoons) garlic powder
45 g (3½ tablespoons) paprika
25 g (5 teaspoons) ground ginger
25 g (5 teaspoons) mango powder

25 g (5 teaspoons) dried mint
25 g (5 teaspoons) beetroot powder
  (deep red colouring)*
20 g (4 teaspoons) chilli powder
10 g (1 teaspoon) anatto seed powder
  (yellow colouring)*

1 Simply mix the ingredients together well, and store.

2 Use as described in the recipes.

*If you use food colouring powder instead use only 5 g red (1 teaspoon) and 3 g sunset yellow (½ teaspoon). These small quantities will achieve a more vibrant colour than beetroot and annatto.

Garam Masala

Garam means hot and masala means mixture of spices, and there are as many combinations and recipes for garam masala as there are cooks who make it. Some use only five or six spices, but I have one recipe which lists as many as 15 spices! This one has only nine and has been my favourite for years. Try it. For the next batch, you might like to vary the mixture to your own preference. That's the fun of Indian cookery. (Again I list in metric only, as that's the way I weigh out the spices for this and it doesn't transfer easily into Imperial.) This particular garam masala is available from The Curry Club (see page 179).

For an *aromatic* garam masala, use this recipe *without* the peppercorns and ginger. I came across a remarkably 'mild' garam masala recipe in Kashmir which uses no hot spices at all. In their place were saffron stamens and rose petals. If you wish to use saffron, add it whole at the very end of cooking.

110 g coriander seeds
110 g cummin seeds
50 g black peppercorns
30 g cassia bark
30 g cloves

30 g brown cardamoms
15 g nutmeg
10 g bay leaves
15 g ground ginger

1 Lightly roast everything except the ground ginger under a low to medium grill or in an oven at about 325°F/160°C/Gas 3. Do not let the spices burn. They should give off a light steam.

2 When they give off an aroma – in the oven, 10 minutes is enough – remove from the heat, cool and grind. A coffee grinder will do if you use small quantities and break up large items first.

3 After grinding add the ground ginger, mix thoroughly and store in an airtight jar. Garam masala will last almost indefinitely, but it is always better to make small fresh batches every few months to get the best flavours.

Panch Phoran

This is a Bengali mixture of five (*panch*) spices. There are several possible combinations. This is my favourite.

Mix together equal parts (a teaspoon of each is plenty) of:

white cummin seeds
fennel seeds
fenugreek seeds

mustard seeds
wild onion seeds

Aromatic Salt

Throughout this book, recipes call for aromatic salt. This is salt, preferably sea salt, to which is added a light spice mixture. Ordinary salt can be used in its place, but the spicing adds a delicacy and subtlety to a recipe. It is a trick I picked up from professional chefs, and I highly recommend it.

Here are two recipes, the first being light and aromatic, the second containing spicier tastes as well as nuts. Finely grind a reasonable size batch and store in a screw-top jar.

Lightly Spiced Salt
100 g (4 oz) coarsely granulated sea salt
1 teaspoon powdered cinnamon
1 teaspoon ground allspice

Spicier Aromatic Salt
1 quantity Lightly Spiced Salt
½ teaspoon ground fenugreek seeds
1 teaspoon dried mint
1 tablespoon ground almonds
½ teaspoon turmeric

MISCELLANEOUS

The following recipes don't strictly come into any of the previous categories, so are headed as above – they're anything but 'miscellaneous' in curry cooking, though!

Ghee

Ghee is a clarified butter, which is very easy to make and gives a distinctive and delicious taste. When cooled and set, it will keep for several months without refrigeration.

If you want to make vegetable ghee, simply use pure vegetable block margarine instead of butter.

2 lb (900 g) any butter

1 Place the butter blocks whole into a medium non-stick pan. Melt at a very low heat.

2 When completely melted, raise heat very slightly. Ensure it does not smoke or burn, but don't stir. Leave to cook for about 1 hour. The impurities will sink to the bottom and float on the top. Carefully skim off the floating sediment with a slotted spoon, but don't touch the bottom.

3 Turn off the heat and allow the ghee to cool a little. Then strain it through kitchen paper or muslin into an airtight storage jar. When it cools it solidifies, although it is quite soft. It should be a bright pale lemon colour and it smells like toffee. If it has burned it will be darker and smell different. Providing it is not too burned it can still be used.

Paneer Cheese

This is a fresh home-made cheese which does not melt when cooked. It is full of protein and easy to make. It resembles compacted cottage cheese and is very common in the sub-continent as a vegetarian dish.

MAKES: about 8 oz (225 g)

4 pints (2·25 litres) full-cream milk
  (not UHT)
4–6 tablespoons any vinegar or lemon
  juice

1 Choose a large pan. If you have one of 12 pint (6·75 litres) capacity, the milk will only occupy a third of the pan and won't boil over (unless the lid is on).

2 Bring the milk slowly to the boil. Add the vinegar or lemon juice, stirring until it curdles – when the curds separate from the whey.

3 Strain into a clean tea towel placed on a strainer over a saucepan. Fold the tea towel over and press through the excess liquid – the whey. Keep for later use as stock.

4 Now place the curds – from now on called paneer – on to the draining board, still in the tea towel. Press it out to a circle about ½ inch (1·25 cm) thick. Place a flat weight (the original saucepan full of water, for instance) on the tea towel and allow it to compress the paneer.

5 If you want crumbly paneer, remove the weight after 30–45 minutes. Crumble the paneer and use as the recipe directs.

6 If you want the paneer to be solid, keep the weight on for 1½–2 hours. Then cut the paneer into cubes.

Deep Fried Paneer

Cubed paneer is normally deep-fried to a pale golden colour for best texture. To do this, heat the deep-fryer to 375°F/190°C and fry the paneer cubes for about 5 minutes.

Coconut

Coconut is used extensively in South India and Bengal and all the curry lands to the East. Desiccated coconut is one substitute for fresh coconut and can be used by adding it dry to your cooking, or by simmering it in water and straining it to create coconut 'milk'. A new product to this country is coconut milk powder – very finely ground dried coconut flesh – which has a creamier taste than desiccated, and mixes well with water.

To choose a fresh coconut, shake before buying to ensure it is full of liquid (the more liquid it has, the fresher it is). Coconuts without liquid or with mouldy or wet eyes should not be used.

1 Make a hole in two of the three eyes with a screwdriver or nail. Drain off and keep the liquid (coconut water).

2 Bake empty coconut in oven at 400°F/200°C/Gas 6 for 15 minutes.

3 While still hot crack it with a hammer. Remove the flesh.

4 Cut into 1 inch (2·5 cm) cubes and soak in water for 4 hours.

5 Strain the flesh, keeping the liquid.

6 Squeeze the flesh to get remaining liquid.

7 Combine the liquids from 1, 5 and 6 to make coconut milk. Use the flesh, in chunks or puréed in curries.

The familiar 7 oz (200 g) rich block of 'creamed coconut' is a combination of freshly grated coconut flesh and coconut oil, which sets solid. To use this boil a little water. Cut off the amount required and melt it in the hot water. If you try to fry it without water, it will burn. It must be kept under refrigeration.

Coconut oil comes set solid in bottles with no instructions as to how to extract it. It is, however, simple. Ensure the cap is screwed on tightly then immerse the bottle in hot water for a few minutes. The oil becomes transparent as it melts.

Onion Tarka

Garnish of Fried Onions

The *tarka* is the traditional crispy brown onion garnish sprinkled over several of the dishes in this book. I like to make a reasonable-sized batch. If cooked correctly these dry crispy pieces will keep, like biscuits, in an airtight tin. To get them crispy, the trick is to dry the onion in a low oven, then to fry at medium heat.

8 oz (225 g) onion
6–8 tablespoons vegetable or
  sunflower oil

1 Finely slice the onions into julienne strips (matchsticks) about $1\frac{1}{2}$ inches (3·75 cm) in length.

2 Pre-heat oven to 210°F/100°C/Gas $\frac{1}{4}$.

3 Spread the onion slices on a baking tray and place in the oven for anything between 30 and 45 minutes.

4 They should now be quite dehydrated, so heat the oil in a karahi or wok.

5 Add the onion slices and stir-fry for 10–15 minutes, until they go dark brown. A little blackening is fine, but control things to prevent an all-black situation.

6 When you have the colour you like, strain off the oil (use it for subsequent cooking).

7 Serve hot or cold.

CHAPTER THREE

Crunchy, Crispy Nibbles

I t is not surprising that, with her culinary tradition stretching back over the centuries, India has invented stupendous and original crispy, crunchy, tasty nibbles. These can be eaten at any time of day or night, but the most appropriate time is with an apéritif (which need not be alcoholic).

At the restaurant or when entertaining, it is a particularly suitable way to settle guests down, relaxing them before the serious business of dining begins. To stimulate the taste buds for the delights to follow, a number of different nibbles can be put on offer. These include a range of spicy crispy 'sticks' called, depending on shape and size, *murukus*, *ganthia* or *sev*. Other crunchy nibbles include *chana dhal* (gram), *kabli chana* (chickpeas), *mattar* (green peas), *mamra* (rice), peanuts, cashews and almonds, *boondi* (deep fried batter drops), *sali* and *jali* (potato straws and crisps).

The raw materials for these delights include nuts, pulses, legumes, rice, various batters and doughs, and the humble potato. Yes, India invented the potato crisp, generations before it became the multi-million dollar best-selling packet snack in the Western world.

Particularly popular are two items to which the West has no commercial answer: Bombay Mix, a delicious mixture of Indian nibbles, and the ubiquitous papadom, that thin flat savoury wafer, without which the Indian meal would be incomplete.

In the pages which follow, we will look at the range of Indian nibbles and how they are made. All these nibbles keep for a long time if kept, like biscuits, in airtight tins. So I like to set aside an afternoon for the job and make large batches of several types of snacks, which keep me in stock for months. Try it! You'll save a fortune and have fun.

Murukus, Ganthia and Sev

Spicy Snacks

These are a family of snacks of different shapes and sizes made from a spicy gram flour dough called *ompadi*. It is the forming of this dough into the various traditional shapes called *murukus* which gives these snacks their uniqueness. A special hand tool called a *murukus* mould press is essential to squeeze the dough through special flat perforated discs known as *ompadi* plates. Each plate is perforated with circular holes or star shapes of different diameters, from tiny to large. The press and its plates are shown in the photograph opposite page 128. They are available from The Curry Club (see Appendices 1 and 2).

The largest shapes are used to make *murukus* which are large star-shaped or plain circular cylinders ranging from about 1 inch (2.5 cm) in diameter and 5 inches (12.5 cm) in length.

Using plates with smaller star-shaped holes creates *ganthia*, which is normally about 1/3 inch (8 mm) in diameter. Plates with small plain circular holes make *sev*. This can range in diameter from 1/3 inch (8 mm) for thick *teekah* *sev* down to $\frac{1}{16}$ inch (1 mm) for very fine *sev*, this latter resembling vermicelli.

In each case the *ompadi* dough is squeezed into deep-frying oil and is cooked, drained, cooled and broken into bite-sized pieces.

Ompadi

Spiced Gram Flour Dough

This dough must be kneaded into a thick cohesive ball, about the same consistency as bread making dough.

MAKES: enough for several uses

7 oz (200g) gram flour
3½ oz (100g) rice flour
2 tablespoons melted ghee
salt
vegetable oil for deep-frying

Spices
1–2 teaspoons chilli powder
1–2 teaspoons ajwain (lovage) seeds
1 teaspoon asafoetida
1 teaspoon turmeric

1 Mix all the ingredients together with sufficient water to make a cohesive ball of dough. The easiest way to do this is to use an electric dough maker.

2 Heat the deep-fryer to 375°F/190°C.

3 Select the *ompadi* plate with the hole size you require and place it into the *murukus* mould press.

4 Fill the press with some of the *ompadi* dough.

5 When the oil is at temperature, hold the press about 4 inches (10 cm) above the surface of the oil and press the dough into the fryer, moving the press around the surface in a slow circular motion. Do not overfill the deep-fryer, i.e. allow enough space for the items to rise and not be cluttered.

6 Fry until the dough crisps up and becomes golden in colour (times vary depending on the thickness being cooked).

7 Remove the batch from the fryer with a slotted spoon. Place on kitchen paper and allow to cool.

8 Repeat stage 4 (changing the plate if you want a different shape) and continue until all the dough is used up.

9 When cool, break the 'sticks' up into bite-sized pieces and store in airtight containers.

Nuts

Raw peanuts, cashews or almonds are used on their own or in Indian snack mixtures. I make a reasonable-sized batch, say 1 lb (around 450 g), and store the different nuts separately in airtight containers.

1 lb (450 g) shelled nuts
about 4 fl oz (100 ml) vegetable oil

1 Heat the oil in a *karahi* or wok.

2 Stir-fry the nuts in 2 or 3 batches for about 5 minutes.

3 Drain off the oil (and re-use it).

4 Store the nuts in airtight containers when cold.

Chana Dhal, Kabli Chana, Mattar and Mamra

Gram Lentils, Chickpeas, Green Peas and Rice Snacks

This group of snacks uses dried ingredients which are soaked, drained, partly dried, deep-fried and spiced. I generally make several types at once, but keep them separate through the entire process.

I normally make a large batch at one time using, say 2 lb (about 900 g) of each item. The technique works for any quantity. Simply adjust the spicing to suit.

MAKES: about 2 lb (900 g)   [V]

2 lb (900 g) dried pulses or peas, or
  rice
vegetable oil for deep-frying

Spices
3–4 tablespoons ground cummin
3–4 tablespoons garam masala
chilli powder to taste
aromatic salt to taste

1 Soak the pulse(s) of your choice, or rice, overnight, then rinse and drain.

2 Spread to dry on kitchen paper or clean tea towels. Leave for about 20 minutes.

3 Meanwhile, heat the deep-fryer to 375°F/190°C.

4 Lower a batch of the damp pulses or rice into the fryer oil until there is a good layer in it.

5 It will whoosh a bit and cook quite fast (normally in less than 5 minutes).

6 Remove the contents with a slotted spoon and place on kitchen paper, allowing it to cool completely.

7 Repeat stages 4 to 6 until all is used up.

8 Then place in an airtight container(s). Throw in the **spices** and shake well. It will keep for several weeks.

Note: If any of these snacks or mixtures becomes stale, simply place on trays in an oven at 225°F/100°C/Gas ¼ for 10 minutes. When it cools it will be crisp again.

Boondi

These are small balls of deep-fried batter made from gram and rice flours and spices. The batter is pushed through a special concave circular perforated steel spoon (called a *chulni* or *poni*). This is about 4 inches (10 cm) in diameter with perforations of about $\frac{3}{16}$ inch (5 mm).

MAKES: about 1½ lb (675 g)   V

12 oz (350 g) gram flour
4 oz (110 g) rice flour
aromatic salt
vegetable oil for deep-frying

Spices
½ teaspoon turmeric
½–2 teaspoons chilli powder

Garnish
4 oz (110 g) fried cashew nuts,
*   chopped*
20 curry leaves
2 teaspoons black mustard seeds,
*   roasted*
2 teaspoons paprika
aromatic salt to taste

1 Mix the two flours, the salt and the **spices** with sufficient water to make a thickish but pourable batter.

2 Allow it to stand whilst you heat the deep-fryer to 350°F/180°C.

3 Beat the batter once more, then put a tablespoon of it onto the *chulni* spoon. It should be thick enough not to drop through the perforations.

4 Hold the *chulni* spoon about 8 inches (20 cm) above the deep-fryer. Then press the batter through the perforations with the back of the tablespoon. The batter should pass through the holes easily to form small balls in the oil. If the batter is too runny it will disintegrate in the oil. If it is rather thick it will form long shapes rather than balls. Adjust the batter accordingly.

5 Repeat stage 4 until the deep-fryer has a well-spaced surface layer of floating *boondis*. Fry for about 5 minutes, turning once or twice.

6 When light golden, remove with a clean perforated spoon. Shake off excess oil and place on kitchen paper. Allow to cool.

7 Repeat stages 4 to 6 until all the *boondis* are cooked.

8 Add the garnish ingredients, mixing them in well, then store the *boondis* in airtight containers and use as required.

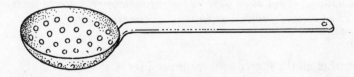

Snack Mixtures

All the above snacks can be eaten as separate entities. Equally they can be mixed in certain ratios to produce mixtures. In the following four popular mixtures all the ingredients (except the specific spices) have been pre-cooked as already described on pages 40–42.

Bombay or Savoury Mix

I am sure that everyone has enjoyed Bombay Mix at one time or another. It is that delicious combination of crispy cooked chickpeas, lentils, nuts, green peas and crunchy savoury 'sticks'. Normally we purchase Bombay Mix and other ready-made snacks in packets of about (3½ oz) 100 g. However, there is no difficulty in making all of these snacks at home. One simply needs a little time, a deep-fryer and the special tool described on page 40. The mixture can be seasoned with chilli powder to any required heat.

MAKES: 4 lb (1.8 kg)   V

All the following cooked as on pages
   40–42:
1 lb (450 g) ganthia
1 lb (450 g) thick (teeka) sev
12 oz (350 g) chana dhal
8 oz (225 g) chickpeas
8 oz (225 g) green peas
4 oz (110 g) peanuts

Spices
6–8 tablespoons garam masala
6–8 tablespoons cummin seeds
2–3 tablespoons ajwain (lovage)
   seeds
chilli powder to taste
aromatic salt to taste

Mix together all the ingredients including the **spices**. Store and use as required.

Dal Mooth

This is a mixture of chana dhal or moong dhal, nuts and spices. In this northern Indian version, almonds are used and it is quite mild. You can use any nuts and add chilli powder if you want to vary it.

MAKES: 2 lb (900 g)   V

1½ lb (675 g) chana or moong dhal or
   combination, cooked as on page 42
8 oz (225 g) almonds, cooked as on
   page 41

1 tablespoon sunflower seeds
1 tablespoon mustard seeds
aromatic salt to taste

Mix together all the ingredients. Store and serve as required.

Chewda, Chevda or Chewra

This mixture is popular all over India, especially in the state of Gujarat where it is particularly enjoyed for its combination of sweet and sour tastes.

MAKES: 2 lb (900g)   V

*1 lb (450g) basmati rice, cooked as
  on page 42
12 oz (350g) split chana dhal,
  cooked as on page 42
3 oz (75g) peanuts, cooked as on
  page 41*

*1 oz (25g) sultanas
24–30 dried curry leaves
2 tablespoons granulated white sugar
1 teaspoon citric acid powder
1 tablespoon aromatic salt*

Mix together all the ingredients. Store and serve as required.

Special Mix

You can create any mixture of your choice by combining anything with anything. Particularly nice, for example, is a combination of Bombay Mix, *Dal Mooth, Chewda, Boondi,* etc.

   This ratio works well, I think.

*2 parts Bombay Mix
1 part Chewda
½ part Dal Mooth
¼ part Boondi
¼ part green peas, cooked as on
  page 42
⅛ part Jali
⅛ part nuts, cooked as on page 41*

Garnish
*roasted cummin seeds to taste
roasted ajwain seeds to taste
aromatic salt to taste
granulated sugar to taste
chilli powder to taste*

Papadoms

The papadom is surely one of India's miracles. The paper-thin circular savoury wafer is as famous as curry itself and no Indian meal would be complete without this divine delight.

Papadoms come in a variety of tastes and spellings – papadoms, pappadams, popadums, pupudums, puppadoms, etc. are just a few literal variants. Sometimes they are called *papads*, but this appears to be a dialectic variation in different parts of India and it does not mean that the papad is in any significant way different from the papadom.

They come in plain unspiced form, and spiced with black pepper, cummin seed, chilli, garlic, whole lentils, etc. Originating in South India, papadoms are normally made from ground lentils. They range in size from 3 inches (7.5 cm) to more than 12 inches (30 cm) in diameter.

Called *appalam*, *happala* and *appadalu* in other parts of South India, they are made by hand, usually by women, who have spent a lifetime learning their skill. A dough is made and the thin discs are slapped out by hand in a trice. The discs are laid out on huge trays and dried in the sun. A practised worker can produce hundreds of identical papadoms each day without the help of any machinery. When they are dried they are packed in dozens or 20s in packets, and it is in this form that most people buy and cook them.

It is possible to make papadoms oneself. However, a little practice will probably be needed to get acceptable results. The dough texture is relatively easy to get right. Rolling into thin discs is not too hard. The absence of sun has to be compensated for by using the oven to dry the papadoms. Please don't be despondent if the results are wanting first or second time around. You will get close eventually.

Plain Papadom

8 oz (225 g) polished urid dhal
½ teaspoon salt
½ teaspoon baking powder
¼ teaspoon asafoetida

4 fl oz (100 ml) mustard or sunflower oil
plain flour

1 Using a coffee grinder, grind about 2 or 3 tablespoons of urid dhal to a fine powder. Use short bursts of power (prolonged grinding will cause it to oil up and go sticky). When fine enough, sieve out any lumps and re-grind.

2 Repeat stage 1 until all the urid dhal is finely ground to a flour.

3 Now a stiff dough must be made. Mix the urid dhal flour, salt, baking powder (this makes the dough 'lighter') and asafoetida with enough water to make a stiff dough. By far the easiest way to do this is to use the dough hook of a food mixer. It is hard work by hand.

4 Leave this stiff dough to stand for an hour or so, then knead it (with the dough hook) and slowly pour in the oil until the dough is soft and pliable.

5 Divide it into 4 equal pieces, then subdivide each of those into 3, so that you have 12 equal-sized lumps. Roll each into a ball.

6 Roll the first ball in plain flour, then roll it out on a floured work surface to obtain a thin circle about 6 inches (15 cm) in diameter. Repeat until you have 12 discs.

7 The next stage in India would be to dry the discs in the sun for a number of hours. This can be simulated by using a plate warmer or oven set at the lowest possible heat (170°F/80°C/Gas $\frac{1}{4}$ or lower).

8 Leave in the oven for at least 2 hours. The papadoms should be moisture-free by then. They will look translucent and be fairly brittle. If they are blotchy give them more time in the oven.

9 Providing they are properly dried, they can be stored in an airtight tin until required for cooking. They may then be either deep-dried, grilled or microwaved as described below.

To Cook

10 To cook, deep-fry the papadoms one at a time (at 340°F/170°C) for about 10 seconds, turning once. Remove from the oil with tongs, shaking off excess. Allow to cool or keep in a warm place for a few hours and each will be crispy and oil-free.

11 Alternatively, cook under the grill. Set the grill tray at a midway position and the heat to about three-quarters. Grill 1 or 2 papadoms at a time for about 10 seconds. Ensure that the edges are cooked. Being oil-free they can be served at once or stored until ready.

12 Papadoms can also be microwaved. Most machines are power rated at 650 watts. Place 2 papadoms in and cook on full power for about 30 seconds. Inspect and apply more heat if necessary. Serve at once or store until needed.

Spicy Papadoms

There a number of spicy variants. These include the following:

finely chopped garlic	*chopped urid dhal*
finely chopped fresh green chilli	*whole cummin seed*
chilli powder	*coarsely ground black pepper*

Add 2–3 teaspoons of one of the above ingredients to the dough mixture towards the end of stage 4 of the plain papadom recipe (opposite and above). The remainder of the method stays the same.

Sali and Jali

Potato Straws and Crisps

These too can be used as nibbles in their own right, or combined with other mixtures. *Sali* are sometimes used to garnish curries, a delicious role for them.

Sali

MAKES: about 1 lb (450 g)   V

4 large potatoes, peeled
vegetable oil for deep-frying

Garnish
1 tablespoon garam masala

½ teaspoon turmeric
0–2 teaspoons chilli powder
aromatic salt to taste

1 Cut the potatoes into thin julienne strips (matchsticks). Spread them on kitchen paper and cover them with it as well, to keep them as dry as possible.

2 Heat the oil in the deep-fryer to 375°F/190°C.

3 Put the potato straws into the pan, a few at a time but quickly, to prevent them from sticking together. When the surface area of the pan is full but not crowded, fry until they stop sizzling and the moisture is cooked out. They will be an attractive golden colour.

4 Remove them from the pan, shaking off excess oil, and place on kitchen paper until cool.

5 Repeat stages 4 and 5 until all the potato straws are cooked and cool.

6 Put them into an airtight container with the garnish spices. Shake well to mix. Store and use as required.

Jali   V

Use the same ingredients and method. The only variation is to cut the potatoes into slices as thin as you can get them. *Jali* are none other than spicy Indian potato crisps.

CHAPTER FOUR

Soups, Starters and Snacks

In many of the curry lands, the concept of the starter does not exist. The meal is not served in a series of courses. Soups, main dishes and desserts are served all together, and the diners choose to eat them in any order they like.

There is, however, a fantastic wealth of superb dishes which can be served as first courses. These include soups, salads, and tasty titbits, all of which make excellent introductions to a meal. I have ranged far and wide for the selection of dishes in this chapter, both in their country of origin and in the choice of main ingredient.

Of particular interest are the starters. They include, amongst other things, fritters, dumplings, pastries, rissoles and crispy items, any of which can be made as snacks or light meals to be enjoyed at any time of day or night.

Shamali Kabul

Afghan Vegetable and Chickpea Soup

Once, when Queen Victoria was Empress, my grandfather was stationed with his British Army regiment in the barren rocky mountain passes of Afghanistan. When they were on the move this simple tasty soup would be waiting for them on arrival at their next camp. This recipe produces a thin soup which, if you prefer, can be strained to give a clear soup. Either way it is highly nutritious.

SERVES: 4   V

2 tablespoons vegetable oil
4 cloves garlic, finely chopped
4 oz (110 g) onion, coarsely chopped
0–4 fresh green chillis, chopped into
   rings
7 oz (200 g) canned tomatoes with
   juice
½ green pepper, finely chopped
1 teaspoon bottled horseradish sauce
7 oz (200 g) cooked chickpeas (page
   66)
1½ pints (900 ml) water or akhni stock
6 spring onions, sliced, including
   leaves
¼ red pepper, cut into strips

2 tablespoons chopped fresh coriander
   leaves
vinegar (any type) to taste
lemon juice to taste
sugar to taste
aromatic salt to taste

Spices (all ground)
½ teaspoon cinnamon
½ teaspoon cummin
½ teaspoon coriander
½ teaspoon turmeric
¼ teaspoon mango powder
¼ teaspoon green cardamom

1 Make a paste of the **spices** by adding water.

2 Heat the oil in a *karahi* or wok. Stir-fry the garlic for 1 minute, add the onion and continue to stir-fry for 5 more minutes. Add the optional chilli and the spice paste and continue to stir-fry for 2–3 more minutes.

3 Transfer the stir-fry mixture to a 4 pint (2.25 litre) saucepan. Add the tomatoes, green pepper, horseradish, chickpeas and water or akhni stock.

4 Bring to the boil, then reduce the heat and allow to simmer for about 10 minutes.

5 Skim off any frothy scum, then add the spring onions, red pepper and fresh coriander. Add vinegar and/or lemon juice and/or sugar and/or salt bit by bit until it is to your taste.

6 Bring back to the boil and serve piping hot.

Golbedako Surwa

Nepalese Tomato Soup

This tasty soup is a favourite of the Ghurka regiment – indeed I obtained this recipe from their Surrey barracks. The Nepalese head chef told me that Sir Edmund Hillary and Sherpa Ten-Singh carried a flask of it to the summit of Everest. I have found it just as good served cold on a hot summer's day, or hot on a cold winter's evening. I prefer to use canned tomatoes for their superb flavour, but fresh ones are equally good provided they are very tasty.

SERVES: 4   V

28 oz (800 g) canned or fresh
  tomatoes
½ pint (300 ml) tomato juice
½ pint (300 ml) water or akhni stock
1 tablespoon tomato ketchup
1 tablespoon tomato purée

chilli powder (optional)
aromatic salt to taste
1–2 teaspoons cummin seeds, roasted
sprinkling chopped fresh coriander
  leaves

1   Put the canned tomatoes with their juice into a 4 pint (2·25 litre) saucepan. If using fresh tomatoes, blanch and skin them first. Add the tomato juice and the water or akhni stock and bring to the boil. Then turn down the heat and simmer for 10 minutes.

2   Whilst it is simmering, add the tomato ketchup and tomato purée and stir in.

3   Add the optional chilli powder and salt to taste.

4   Garnish with the cummin seeds and fresh coriander and serve.

Chin-Hin

Burmese Sour Soup

This soup is one of Burma's favourites. It should be very clear and thin like a consommé and the herbs and lettuce should be briefly cooked to retain their shape and colour.

SERVES: 4   V

2 tablespoons vegetable oil
2–4 cloves garlic, puréed
4 oz (110 g) onion, cut into short thin
  slices
½ teaspoon turmeric
2 pints (1·2 litres) water or akhni
  stock
1 tablespoon tomato purée

1 tablespoon tamarind purée or fresh
  lemon juice
2 shakes soy sauce
aromatic salt or sea salt to taste
ground black pepper
1 bunch watercress leaves
a few leaves of sorrel or purslane
a few leaves of lettuce heart

1 Heat the oil in a *karahi* or wok. Stir-fry the garlic, onion and turmeric for about 5 minutes.

2 Transfer this mixture to a 4 pint (2.25 litre) saucepan. Add the water or akhni stock and tomato purée. Bring to the boil, then reduce the heat and simmer for 10–15 minutes.

3 Add the tamarind or lemon juice, soy sauce and salt and black pepper to taste (my quantities are guides only). Bring back to a simmer.

4 Prior to serving, add the watercress, sorrel or purslane and lettuce leaves. Once the soup re-simmers, serve immediately.

Tom Liang Kaeng

Spicy Thai Vegetable Soup

One of Thailand's most celebrated soups is called Tom Liang Kaeng and it contains huge juicy prawns. This version replaces the prawns with vegetables, but non-vegetarians could add 10–12 prawns along with the radishes in stage 2. Thai soups include a unique combination of spices, savoury tastes and fragrances, the latter from the herbs used. This soup is quite runny but the coconut milk makes it opaque and thicker than consommé.

SERVES: 4   V

2 tablespoons sunflower or vegetable oil
2–4 cloves garlic, finely chopped
4 oz (110 g) onion, finely chopped
2 inch (5 cm) cube galingale or fresh ginger, shredded
0–4 fresh green or red chillies, chopped (optional)
1¾ pints (1 litre) water

4–6 dried lime leaves
4 stalks fresh or 2 tablespoons dried lemon grass
6 oz (175 g) mooli (white radish), shredded
10–12 red radishes, sliced
2 oz (50 g) coconut milk powder
6–8 fresh basil leaves, chopped
some sprigs coriander leaves

1 Heat the oil in a *karahi* or wok. Stir-fry the garlic, onion and galingale or ginger for 5 minutes. Add the chillies (optional) and continue to stir-fry for 2 more minutes.

2 Transfer the stir-fry to a 4 pint (2·25 litre) saucepan. Add the water and bring to the boil, then reduce the heat to a simmer. Add the lime leaves, lemon grass, mooli and radishes. Simmer for 8–10 minutes.

3 Mix the coconut powder with water to make a runny paste. Add it to the soup with the basil at the end of stage 2 and simmer for a few more minutes.

4 Garnish with the fresh coriander and serve.

Kari Sop

Singapore Curry Lentil and Vegetable Soup

Singapore is a great melting pot of cultures and cuisines, being home to Chinese, Malayan, Indonesian and Indian communities and their food. This recipe came from one of the celebrated food stalls at Telok Ayer Market. They served it with Indian bread and, believe me, very filling it was. It should be fairly thick (of pouring consistency), but it can be simply thinned to your taste by adding more water.

SERVES: 4   V

2 oz (50 g) red lentils (masoor)
2 tablespoons vegetable oil or ghee
2 cloves garlic, finely chopped
4 oz (110 g) onion, finely chopped
1 tablespoon curry paste
1¼ pints (750 ml) water or akhni stock

4 oz (110 g) fresh or frozen mixed
* diced vegetables (e.g. peas, carrot,*
* sweetcorn, green beans, etc.)*
salt to taste
garam masala
chopped fresh coriander leaves

1 Soak the lentils in plenty of cold water for at least an hour, then rinse.

2 Heat the oil or ghee in a *karahi* or wok and stir-fry the garlic, onion and curry paste for 5 minutes.

3 Transfer the stir-fry to a 4 pint (2·25 litre) saucepan. Add the water or akhni stock and the lentils and bring to the boil. Reduce the heat and simmer for about 20 minutes. Remove any frothy scum.

4 At the end of that time, test to ensure that the lentils are cooked. Add the vegetables and simmer for 5 more minutes. Add salt to taste. (Add more water if you wish to thin the soup, bringing it back to a simmer.)

5 Serve garnished with a sprinkling of garam masala and fresh coriander.

Batata Pava

Gujarati Potato Snack

The state of Gujarat, north of Bombay, produces one of India's foremost vegetarian cuisines. Their food is very mild and they enjoy sweet tastes. *Batata pava* is a mixture of small potato cubes mixed with coconut, spices, puffed basmati rice (*mamra*) and sugar. It is served cold and becomes chewy, crispy and extraordinarily tasty when combined with two traditional sauces: tamarind (brown and sour) and chilli (green and hot).

SERVES: 4   V

2 tablespoons vegetable oil
8 oz (225 g) potatoes, peeled, boiled and diced into $\frac{1}{4}$ inch (8 mm) cubes
juice of 1 lemon
1 tablespoon chopped fresh coriander leaves
1 teaspoon brown sugar
$\frac{1}{2}$–2 green chillies (to taste), chopped
1 tablespoon grated fresh or desiccated coconut

salt to taste
4 oz (100 g) mamra (puffed basmati rice)

Spices
$\frac{1}{2}$ teaspoon mustard seeds
$\frac{1}{2}$ teaspoon turmeric
$\frac{1}{4}$ teaspoon asafoetida

1   Heat the oil in a *karahi* or wok. Stir-fry the **spices** for 1 minute, then add all the other ingredients except the *mamra*. Stir-fry until hot.

2   Toss in the *mamra* at the last minute to keep it crisp. Serve cold, accompanied with the two sauces in separate serving bowls (see below).

Brown Sauce (sweet and sour)

4 oz (110 g) tamarind purée
4 oz (110 g) dried dates, stoned

4 oz (110 g) brown sugar
1 teaspoon ground cummin

Grind the ingredients in a blender or food processor to a thick, smooth sauce.

Green Sauce (hot)

2 oz (50 g) roasted chana snack ($\frac{1}{2}$ packet)
1 oz (25 g) raw peanuts

1 oz (25 g) fresh green chillies, chopped
1 fl oz (25 ml) vinegar (any type)

Grind the above ingredients as for Brown Sauce.

Chaat Paapri Ke Gol Goppa

Potato Snack with Crunchy Wafers

This is one of those fabulous snacks for which India is renowned, although it is little known outside India. It originates from Gujarat, where it will be found at street stalls. I obtained this recipe from Sat Gupta, a Gujarati school teacher now living in Southall. Years ago he taught me a very great deal about the skills of Indian cookery. The preparation really is easy. It is in several parts: the potato curry, the chutneys, the drink and the small crunchy wafers (*gol goppas*). I like to make a good quantity of the wafers and store them in an airtight tin where they keep for ages, like biscuits. This dish is served cold and is one of Sat's favourites.

SERVES: 4   V

Potato Curry
1 lb (450 g) potatoes, peeled and
  boiled
2 tablespoons curry paste
1 tablespoon chopped fresh coriander
  leaves
1 tablespoon chopped fresh or dried
  mint

The Drink (jal jeera)
$\frac{1}{2}$ pint (300 ml) water
1 teaspoon black Indian salt or sea
  salt
1 teaspoon brown sugar
1 teaspoon ground cummin
$\frac{1}{2}$ teaspoon chilli powder (optional)
shake of Worcestershire sauce
crushed ice

The Wafers (gol goppa)
1 lb (450 g) strong white flour
3 tablespoons vegetable oil
1 teaspoon salt

The Chutneys and Pickles
natural yoghurt (not suitable for
  vegans)
Vinegared Onion Rings
Gasneech or Mooli Chatni
Chaat or Garjar Am

Garnishes
salad
lemon or lime wedges
roasted cummin seeds
mango powder
garam masala
aromatic salt
chilli powder (optional)

Potato Curry

1 Allow the potatoes to cool after cooking, then dice into $\frac{1}{4}$ inch (8 mm) cubes.

2 Mix in the other ingredients and chill in the refrigerator until required.

The Drink

3 Mix together all the ingredients except the ice. Put into a jug and chill in the refrigerator until required.

4 Add the crushed ice prior to serving.

The Wafers

5 Mix the ingredients into a pliable dough (see page 140 for general dough making method).

6 Take a marble-sized piece of dough.

7 Roll it into a thin disc about $1\frac{1}{2}$ inch (3.75 cm) in diameter.

8 Repeat stages 6 and 7 until all the dough is used up.

9 Heat the deep-fryer to a minimum of 190°C/375°F.

10 Place a wafer into the oil. If the oil is hot enough, it will puff up like a toad. Add the next wafer and continue until the fryer can take no more. Turn each disc once and remove them, if possible in the order you put them in, after a couple of minutes.

11 Drain them and place on kitchen paper to cool.

12 Repeat stages 10 and 11 until all the discs are done.

13 When cold the wafers will become very crispy and crunchy. Serve at once or store in an airtight container.

To Serve the Dish

14 This dish is served cold, ideally on a thali tray with several small *katori* bowls (see Glossary). Alternatively, give each person a dinner plate with small serving bowls.

15 Garnish the tray or plate with a small salad and some lemon or lime wedges. Put about 8 wafers on the tray. Put the potato curry into a larger individual bowl and sprinkle the garnish spices over it. Serve the yoghurt, onion, tamarind and mint chutneys in individual small bowls. Serve the drink in individual tumblers.

Kra Tong Thong

Crispy Cups with a Spicy Filling

This simple starter from Thailand has a garlicky and highly spiced filling. Reduce the garlic if that does not appeal, but keep the spice level the same – that's what makes it so good. The filling is placed inside a rice flour crispy cup, which must be made first from a batter dough rolled out and deep fried. The easy way round this is to use rice paper discs, available in packets.

SERVES: 4

For the Cups
16 rice paper discs about 5 inches
   12.5 cm) in diameter

The Filling
6 oz (175 g) raw peanuts
2 tablespoons sesame oil
6 teaspoons garlic purée
4 tablespoons onion purée
2 eggs
4 spring onions with leaves,
   chopped

2 tablespoons chopped fresh coriander
   leaves
2 oz (50 g) mashed potato
salt

Spices
2 teaspoons ground coriander
2 teaspoons ground cummin
1 teaspoon turmeric
1 teaspoon chilli powder
½ teaspoon lemon grass powder
½ teaspoon galingale powder

1 Roast the peanuts by spreading them out on the grill pan and applying medium grill heat for 2–3 minutes. Allow to cool.

2 When cold, grind them to a coarse powder in a food processor by pulsing the machine on and off.

3 Heat the oil in a *karahi* or wok and stir-fry the garlic and onion purées for about 2 minutes.

4 Add the peanuts, eggs, spring onions and fresh coriander and stir-fry until the eggs set. Add the **spices** and the mashed potato and sufficient water to prevent the mixture from being dry but keeping it stiff and mouldable. Add salt to taste and allow to cool.

5 Preheat the deep-fryer to 375°F/190°C. Place a heaped teaspoon of filling into the centre of a rice paper disc. Repeat with the remaining 15 discs.

6 Carefully fold the first disc up into a purse or cup shape and, holding it with tongs, gently immerse it into the deep-fryer. Keep holding it until it goes golden (it only takes a few seconds). Remove and place on kitchen paper. Repeat with the remaining 15 discs.

7 Allow them to get cold (but do not refrigerate them) and they will become very crispy. Serve cold within 1 hour.

Spicy Chestnuts

If you adore chestnuts, this little dish may appeal. It is possible to buy them vacuum packed, frozen or (the least preferable) canned at all times of the year. Try this dish as a starter or as an accompaniment with the main course.

SERVES: 4   V

12 oz (350 g) cooked, peeled chestnuts
1 teaspoon ginger purée
1 teaspoon brown sugar
1 tablespoon curry paste

Garnish
1 tablespoon chopped fresh coriander

1 Mix all the ingredients together in a pan and warm through.

2 Garnish with the fresh coriander and serve.

Q'root

Savoury Yoghurt

Pronounced *kroot*, this is an Afghani dish. *Q'root* is strained yoghurt which is pressed and dried into hard white marbles. These keep indefinitely and are reconstituted with water when required.

A favourite way of eating *q'root* is to combine it with salt, pepper, garlic and mint. In this recipe I am using yoghurt, cream cheese or cottage cheese and soured cream to create a thick and creamy texture. Use *q'root* as a starter, snack, dip or chutney.

SERVES: 4

5 fl oz (150 ml) Greek or strained
  yoghurt
5 fl oz (150 ml) cream cheese or
  cottage cheese
5 fl oz (150 ml) soured cream

1–2 cloves garlic, finely chopped
1 teaspoon ground black pepper
$\frac{1}{2}$ teaspoon aromatic salt
chopped fresh or dried mint

1 Mix the yoghurt with the cream cheese or cottage cheese and soured cream, beating briskly. Add the garlic, pepper and salt.

2 Serve in individual bowls garnished with the mint. Chill in the refrigerator for a minimum of 2 hours before serving.

Bhare Avocado Ka Sootimolee

Stuffed Avocado with Asparagus

I greatly enjoy experimenting with non-traditional Indian ingredients combined with very traditional spicings. This dish is a good example. It uses a small portion of leftover rice, Cheddar cheese, soured cream, mayonnaise, spices and two succulent vegetables which, apart from the great Indian hotel restaurants, do not appear in the Indian repertoire: avocado and asparagus. It is very simple to make and it is, in my view, a very elegant starter, combining East with West in a satisfying way.

SERVES: 4

*16 asparagus shoots (French white is
  the most succulent)*
2 oz (50 g) Cheddar cheese
*1 cupful pre-cooked (spiced or plain)
  basmati rice*
1 small carton soured cream
1 tablespoon mayonnaise
2 tablespoons tandoori paste

aromatic salt to taste
2 ripe avocado pears

Garnish
paprika or chilli powder
finely chopped parsley
4 pieces red capsicum pepper
salad leaves
lemon or lime wedges

1 The asparagus must be cooked in advance. As the tips are delicate, steaming is best. In fact a fish steamer is perfect for the job. If you do not have a steamer, place a strainer above the boiling water in a saucepan. Steam for about 10 minutes. Remove and cool. Chill in the refrigerator for at least 2 hours.

2 Grate the Cheddar cheese.

3 Plan to have some leftover cooked cold rice to hand. It doesn't matter whether it is spiced or plain, but remove any whole spices.

4 Mix the rice with the cheese, soured cream, mayonnaise and tandoori paste. This gives an attractive pink mixture, which should be stiff enough to shape. Add salt to taste and keep chilled until required.

5 No more than 1 hour before serving, halve the avocados and stone them. Press them down slightly on a work surface, so that they will not roll when stuffed.

6 Carefully place enough filling onto an avocado half to fill the hole and cover the surface completely, and build it up to a rounded mould.

7 Repeat with the other 3 halves.

8 Garnish with a sprinkling of paprika or chilli powder, parsley and a longish piece of red pepper, shaped in any way that pleases you (a cock's comb is fun).

9 Return the loaded avocados to the refrigerator until required.

10 To serve, place an avocado half on a plate in a nest of salad leaves with the asparagus alongside. Add a wedge of lemon or lime. Finger bowls are advisable.

Note: Freeze any spare filling or incorporate it in a subsequent curry.

Gado Gado

Traditional Indonesian Salad

This salad appears with many variations in Malaya and Indonesia. It usually includes bean sprouts, with a selection of other vegetables – I use equal quantities of cucumber, carrot, white radish, Chinese leaves, and red cabbage. Potato, beans and fried tofu can be added or substituted.

The traditional presentation requires each item to be equally and attractively distributed around a serving plate. A spicy sauce is served in a gravy boat (hot or cold) and the diners choose the ingredients of their choice and pour the sauce over them.

SERVES: 4

The Salad
4 inch (10 cm) piece cucumber
2 large carrots
4 inch (10 cm) piece mooli (white radish)
top head of Chinese leaves
2–3 oz (50g–75 g) red cabbage
4 oz (110 g) bean sprouts
5 hard-boiled quail's eggs

Garnish
watercress or other herbs

The Sauce
4 oz (110 g) raw peanuts
2 tablespoons vegetable oil
2–4 teaspoons garlic purée
4 oz (110 g) onion purée
2 tablespoons vinegar (any type)
2 tablespoons brown sugar
1–3 tablespoons lemon grass powder
2 oz (50 g) coconut milk powder
½ teaspoon salt

The Salad

1 Cut the cucumber into matchstick pieces. Shred the carrot and the white radish and finely chop the Chinese leaves and the red cabbage. Wash the bean sprouts.

2 Arrange these items on the serving plate in six equal segments. Cut each egg in half and arrange decoratively on the plate. Garnish with the watercress or herbs. Chill in the refrigerator for up to 2 hours.

The Sauce

3 Roast the peanuts by spreading them out on the grill pan and applying medium grill heat for 2–3 minutes. Allow to cool.

4 When cold, grind them to a coarse powder in a food processor by pulsing the machine on and off.

5 Heat the oil in a *karahi* or wok. Stir-fry the garlic and onion for 2 minutes. Add the remaining ingredients, including the ground peanuts, and sufficient water to make a thickish paste. Stir-fry for about 5 minutes.

6 Add more water if you want the sauce thinner. Serve hot or cold with the salad.

Kachu Paka

Raw Vegetable Salad

We have already met two remarkable dishes from the Indian state of Gujarat. Here is another of equal excellence. Usually the cabbage and spinach are blanched and cooled, but by keeping them raw the texture is made more robust and crunchy, and I think it is much more interesting.

SERVES: 4   V

1½ oz (40 g) whole black urid dhal
¼ white cabbage and/or red cabbage
8 spinach leaves
4–6 spring onions
2 tablespoons sunflower or light oil
2 tablespoons watercress
2 tablespoons fresh coriander leaves
2 cloves garlic, finely chopped
2–3 tablespoons grated fresh coconut

2 teaspoons white sugar (optional)
aromatic salt to taste

Spices
1 teaspoon sesame seeds
1 teaspoon mustard seeds
½ teaspoon cummin seeds
½ teaspoon lovage seeds

1 Soak the dhal in ample water for at least 6 hours, then rinse and drain.

2 Wash and trim the vegetables.

3 Finely shred the cabbage, coarsely chop the spinach, spring onions, watercress and fresh coriander and mix them in a bowl.

4 Heat the oil in a *karahi* or wok. Stir-fry the **spices** for 1 minute. Add the garlic and stir-fry for 1 more minute. Add the drained dhal and stir-fry for about 3 minutes. Remove from the heat and cool.

5 When cold, mix the stir-fry in the bowl with the remaining ingredients. Add salt to taste. Chill in the refrigerator for 2 hours prior to serving.

Kumbi Ka Soonf Salat

Mushroom and Fennel Salad

Salads in India are infrequently encountered. They simply are not part of the Indian culinary tradition. However, spicy salads make excellent starters and they are delicious. I encountered this combination at the magnificent *Oberoi Grand Hotel* in Calcutta. No cooking is required, just a short marination.

SERVES: 4   V

8–10 oz (225–300 g) small white
  button mushrooms
1 bulb fresh fennel
4 stalks celery
1 clove garlic, finely chopped
½ inch (1.5 cm) cube fresh ginger,
  finely chopped
4 tablespoons walnut or hazelnut oil

1 teaspoon garam masala
1 teaspoon panch phoran
aromatic salt to taste

Garnish
lettuce leaves
fresh lemon or lime juice
sprigs of fresh coriander or parsley

1 Wash the vegetables. Keep the mushrooms whole and coarsely chop the fennel and the celery.

2 Mix all the ingredients in a salad bowl and allow to marinate for about 2 hours in the refrigerator.

3 Serve cold, of course, on a nest of lettuce leaves. Sprinkle over the lemon or lime juice and garnish with the fresh coriander or parsley. This salad goes well with fresh hot chupattis (page 147).

The eight colour photographs in this book take us on a culinary journey through the many curry lands.

Opposite, dishes from *Singapore, Indonesia and Malaysia*   Clockwise from top: Gado Gado with peanut sauce in separate dish (page 62), Goreng Pisang (page 177), Achar Kunning (page 170), Sayurmi Kari (page 98), Buah Tomat (page 169), Pakari (page 90)

Facing page 65, dishes from *Thailand*   Top to bottom: Mee Krob (page 97), Nam Prik (in small dish next to teapot, page 166), Tom Liang Kaeng (page 53), Swan Garnish (page 123), Khao Niaw Man (page 176), Khao Phed (page 138) with Taeng Kwah Yam (page 167)

Laala Phalia Ka Til Salat

Red Vegetables and Sesame Salad

Here is another unusual and totally original salad. I came across it at a party given by an Indian business family in Cochin, in southern India. The dish was the innovation of the man of the household, who enjoys experimenting with new combinations. The point about it is that it uses all red vegetables, so that it is very vibrant and attractive when served. It makes an excellent starter.

SERVES: 4   V

2 tablespoons sesame oil
2–4 cloves garlic, finely chopped
4 oz (110 g) carrot
1 medium-sized beetroot, cooked
1 stick rhubarb
1 red capsicum pepper
1 medium-sized red onion
16 cherry tomatoes
4 fresh red chillies (optional)
2–4 tablespoons walnut oil
1 tablespoon brown sugar

1–2 tablespoons wine or herbal
  vinegar
aromatic salt to taste

Garnish
1 radicchio (red chicory)
finely chopped parsley
4 wedges of lemon or lime

Spices
4 tablespoons sesame seeds
2 tablespoons mustard seeds
1 teaspoon cummin seeds

1 Heat the sesame oil in a *karahi* or wok. Stir-fry the **spices** for 1 minute, then add the garlic and stir-fry for a minute more. Remove from the heat and cool.

2 Wash all the vegetables, removing unwanted matter, then prepare as follows: shred the carrot (Indian carrots are a deep red colour, but our standard orange ones look just as good); dice the beetroot into $\frac{1}{4}$ inch (8 mm) cubes; cut the rhubarb into small chunks and the red pepper into small diamond shapes; cut the red onion into rings and leave the cherry tomatoes and the optional red chillies whole.

3 When it is cold, transfer the stir-fry and the prepared vegetables to a bowl and mix well. Add the walnut oil, sugar, vinegar and salt to taste. Put the bowl in the refrigerator and chill for 2–4 hours.

4 Serve cold, of course, in a nest of radicchio leaves, garnished with parsley and neat lemon or lime wedges.

Rajma Plus Salat

Beans and Chickpea Salad

Cape Cormorun, on the very tip of southern India, is where the Arabian Sea meets the Indian Ocean. On a recent Curry Club gourmet tour our schedule took us to the Cape. A special picnic had been prepared by the chefs at the *Ashok Kovalam Beach Resort Hotel* a few miles up the coast. It contained a number of tantalising cold dishes, one of which I reproduce here.

SERVES: 4   V

*4 oz (110 g) red kidney beans
  (rajma)
4 oz (110 g) black-eyed beans (lobia)
4 oz (110 g) whole chickpeas (kabli
  chana)
2 tablespoons sesame oil
2–4 cloves garlic, finely chopped
1 inch (2.5 cm) cube fresh ginger,
  shredded
4 oz (110 g) onion, finely chopped
0–2 fresh green chillies (optional)
1 teacupful fresh coriander leaves,
  chopped
aromatic salt to taste
lime or lemon juice*

*Spices 1 (ground)
1 teaspoon coriander
1 teaspoon garam masala
½ teaspoon turmeric
½ teaspoon mango powder*

*Spices 2 (whole, roasted)
2 teaspoons mustard seeds
1½ teaspoons cummin seeds
½ teaspoon wild onion seeds*

1 Soak the beans and chickpeas overnight in separate bowls with ample water.

2 Next day, rinse each thoroughly and, still keeping them separate, boil them in ample water until they are tender. They will each take different amounts of time; the chickpeas taking longest, so keep testing after about 35 minutes.

3 When they are cooked, rinse in cold water, drain and combine.

4 Heat the oil in a *karahi* or wok and stir-fry the garlic, ginger, onion and optional chillies for about 5 minutes. Add **spices 1** and stir-fry them in for a further couple of minutes.

5 Add a small amount of water to keep mixture loose, then add the beans and chickpeas, **spices 2** and half the fresh coriander. Mix well, remove from the heat and add salt to taste.

6 When cold, transfer to a bowl and refrigerate for between 1 and 4 hours. To serve, garnish with coriander and a squeeze of lime or lemon juice.

Hara Mattar Pati
•
Green Pea and Mashed Potato Rissoles

This recipe is the combination of spices with mashed potatoes and peas, which I obtained from a catering school in Delhi. These sausage-shaped rissoles are rolled in breadcrumbs and deep-fried.

MAKES: 8 rissoles   V

8 oz (225 g) cooked or thawed frozen
  peas, partly mashed
8 oz (225 g) mashed potato
1 teaspoon aromatic salt
vegetable oil for deep-frying
breadcrumbs

Spices
1 teaspoon ground cummin
1 teaspoon ground coriander
1 teaspoon garam masala
½ teaspoon ajwain (lovage) seeds
1 teaspoon chilli powder (optional)

1 Mix the cold peas, mashed potato, salt and **spices** together to create a mouldable mixture.

2 Divide the mixture into 8 equal-sized portions and mould them into sausage shapes.

3 Heat the deep-fryer to 170°F/340°C.

4 Whilst it is heating up, roll each rissole in ample breadcrumbs.

5 Deep-fry the rissoles for about 10 minutes.

6 Serve hot as a snack or to accompany a main meal. They can also be cooled and frozen, then reheated as required.

Spicy Potato Rissoles

In this variation of the previous recipe, the peas are omitted, nuts are added, and the spice combination is slightly altered. The shape this time is a round disc about 2½ inches (6 cm) in diameter.

MAKES: 8 rissoles   V

1 lb (450 g) mashed potato
2 oz (50 g) almonds or cashew nuts,
  chopped
1 teaspoon aromatic salt

Spices
2 teaspoons garam masala
1 teaspoon ground coriander
½ teaspoon cummin seeds
1 teaspoon chilli powder (optional)

Follow the method for the previous recipe, substituting the nuts for the peas and changing the shape as described above.

Philourie
Spicy Vegetable Fritters

These fritters are one of the highlights of the Indian snack repertoire. I make no apology that they are high in calories – they are too delicious for an apology. Called *philourie* in southern India, *bhajia* in Bengal and Bangladesh and *pakora* in northern India, when freshly cooked they are a beautiful golden colour. They should be very light and very tasty. To achieve this the following observations must be adhered to:

1 No less than 50% of the flour used must be gram flour.
2 The batter must not be too wet.
3 The fritters must be deep-fried. Shallow frying makes them stodgy.
4 The oil temperature must be 190°C/375°F (the same as for chip frying).
5 The 'filling' ingredient must be raw for optimum crispness.

The batter is combined with any filling of your choice. The most common, and my favourite, is onion, but you can use any alternative. Some suggestions include potato, aubergine, carrot, turnip, parsnip or mooli (all best shredded). Small cauliflower florets, mushrooms, peppers and chillies work well. So do paneer cubes. Dry or fresh fruit is excellent. I once had some amazing apple *philouries* in Mysore.

There are innumerable recipes for the batter. Here are three (one of them vegan). Each has a subtle difference. You might like to try each one, then perhaps try combinations to create your own preference. This method gives irregular-shaped fritters.

MAKES: 8 philourie

Batter 1
4 oz (110 g) gram flour (besan) or
2 oz (50 g) gram flour and 2 oz
(50 g) plain flour
1 egg
3 oz (75 g) natural yoghurt
1 tablespoon fresh or bottled lemon
juice
1 teaspoon salt
½ teaspoon lovage seeds (ajwain)
2 teaspoons garam masala
2 teaspoons dried fenugreek leaves
½–2 teaspoons chilli powder

Batter 2 V
4 oz (110 g) gram flour (besan) or 2 oz
(50 g) gram flour and 2 oz (50 g)
plain flour
1 egg
1 teaspoon ginger purée
1 teaspoon garlic purée
3 fl oz (85 ml) vinegar (any type)
3 teaspoons cummin seeds
1½ teaspoons ground coriander
½ teaspoon mango powder
½ teaspoon garam masala
½–2 teaspoons chilli powder
1 teaspoon salt

Batter 3   V

4 oz (110 g) gram flour (besan)
2 tablespoons chopped fresh coriander
  leaves
1 tablespoon curry paste
1 teaspoon garam masala
1 teaspoon ground cummin
a pinch of asafoetida (hing)
1 teaspoon salt
sufficient water to make a thick batter

Filling

8 oz (225 g) onion (1 large Spanish
  onion), chopped into fine 1 inch
  (2.5 cm) strips or 8 oz (225 g) any
  ingredient or combination of your
  choice as mentioned in the
  introduction
vegetable oil for deep-frying

1 Mix the batter ingredients to achieve a thickish paste which will drop sluggishly off the spoon. Let it stand for at least 10 minutes, during which time the mixture will absorb the moisture.

2 Next add your principal filling ingredient(s). Mix in well and leave again for about 10 minutes to absorb the batter mixture.

3 Meanwhile, heat the deep-frying oil to 375°F/190°C. This temperature is below smoking point and will cause a sliver of batter to splutter a bit, then float more or less at once.

4 Inspect the mixture. There must be no 'powder' left. It must be well mixed. Then simply scoop out $\frac{1}{8}$ of the mixture and place it carefully in the oil. Place all 8 portions in, but allow about 30 seconds between each one so the oil will maintain its temperature.

5 Fry for 10 minutes, turning once. Remove from the oil, drain well and serve with salad garnishes, lemon wedges and chutneys.

Boolani Gadana

Fried Leeks Encased in Pastry

We return to Afghanistan for these very tempting pastries. Traditionally half-moon shaped, they appear on special occasions such as weddings and birthdays, but of course they are excellent at any time. There are two types: *boolani gadana* has a leek filling; *boolani katchalu* contains spicy mashed potato. Being deep-fried, they are best fresh, when they melt in the mouth, but they can be served cold. They can also be frozen after cooking and reheated in the oven.

MAKES: 16 boolani   V

The Filling
2 leeks
4 spring onions
6 tablespoons vegetable oil
1 tablespoon garlic purée
1 tablespoon onion purée
0–2 fresh green chillies, chopped
  (optional)
1 tablespoon tomato purée
aromatic salt to taste

Spices
1 teaspoon ground cassia bark
1 teaspoon ground cummin
½ teaspoon ground green cardamom
½ teaspoon ground clove

The Pastry
1 lb (450 g) strong white flour or ata
  flour (for brown version)

vegetable oil for deep-frying

The Filling

1 Wash the leeks carefully, ensuring that the grit and soil is cleaned from between the leaves. Discard the dead part of the leaves, then finely chop the remainder.

2 Chop the spring onions in the same way.

3 Heat the oil in a *karahi* or wok. Stir-fry the garlic and onion purées for 3 or 4 minutes. Add the **spices** and continue for a couple of minutes more. Add the leeks, spring onions, optional chillies and tomato purée. Simmer and stir-fry for 10 minutes. Add salt to taste. Put the mixture into a strainer to remove excess oil (which can be re-used in another spicy dish) and allow to cool.

The Pastry

4 Make a pliable dough by mixing water with the flour (see page 140 for general dough making recipe).

5 When it is ready, divide it into 16 balls and roll out each ball into a disc about 4 inches (10 cm) in diameter.

6 Heat the deep-fryer to 375°F/190°C.

7 Put about 1–1½ tablespoons of filling into one half of a disc, but do not over fill it or it will burst during cooking.

8 Fold the disc in half and press the rims together firmly.

9 Repeat stages 3 and 4 with the remaining 15 discs.

10 Place a boolani into the oil. As soon as it starts to float, add a second. Do this until 4 are frying (don't cook more than 4 at a time or you will overload the fryer, thus reducing the temperature).

11 When they are golden (after about 10 minutes) remove them, shaking off excess oil, and rest them on kitchen paper. Keep them in a warmer if necessary.

12 Repeat stages 7 and 8 until all are cooked.

13 Serve hot and fresh with chutneys and salad, or cold. When cold they can be frozen.

Note: Freeze any spare filling or incorporate it into another curry dish.

Boolani Katchalu   V

Substitute 6 oz (175 g) mashed potato for the leeks in the preceding recipe. All the other ingredients and the **spices** are the same. Follow the method from stage 2, adding the potato with the spring onions, optional chillies and tomato purée.

Patra

Cabbage Roll

I suppose the best way to describe this dish is to say that it is like a Swiss roll, where a flat sponge is spread with jam, rolled up into a cylinder and cut into slices to serve. In the case of *patra*, large cabbage leaves are spread with spicy thick batter. They are then rolled up to produce cylinders of about 3 inches (7.5 cm) in diameter, then baked and, when cooked, sliced and served hot as a snack or an accompaniment to curries.

This Gujarati speciality is well worth the minimal effort it takes to make.

SERVES: 4   [V]

The Paste
3 oz (75 g) gram flour
2 teaspoons garlic purée
2 tablespoons lemon juice
1 teaspoon mustard seed
½ teaspoon cummin seed
¼ teaspoon asafoetida (optional)
2–4 fresh green chillies (optional),
   finely chopped
aromatic salt to taste

The Leaves
8 soft spring cabbage or colcasia
   leaves, each about 8 inches (20 cm)
   long after stalks are removed
6 spinach leaves
vegetable oil for shallow-frying

1 Make up the paste by mixing the ingredients with enough water to form a thick batter.

2 Wash the cabbage or colcasia leaves.

3 Do the same with the spinach leaves.

4 Blanch them all in boiling water for about 2 minutes to soften. Drain and cool.

5 Spread out the cabbage or colcasia leaves on a work surface overlapping each by about 3 inches (7·5 cm) (see diagram 1).

6 Spread the paste across the leaves as shown in diagram 1.

7 Fold over the tips of the leaves and the sides, pressing them onto the batter to create a rectangle about 10 inches (25 cm) by 6 inches (10 cm) (see diagram 2). Cover these tips with a little more batter, then place the spinach leaves on top, keeping them within the rectangle and cutting them to fit as necessary.

8 Smear a little more paste over the top surface, then roll up the rectangle like a Swiss roll. Use a dollop of paste to seal the end (see diagram 3).

9 Place the rolls seal side down in a steamer and steam for about $\frac{1}{2}$ hour.

10 Allow to cool (overnight in the fridge if you wish), then cut into slices about $\frac{1}{2}$ inch (1·25 cm) thick.

11 Just prior to serving, shallow-fry each slice for a couple of minutes on each side. Serve hot as a snack or as an accompaniment with a main meal.

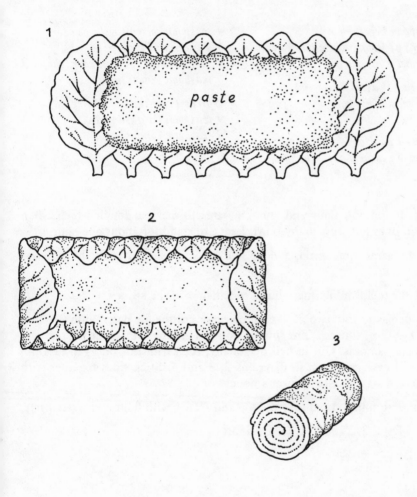

Samosa

The samosa is a familiar friend to all those who enjoy Indian cuisine. It is a triangular pastry with a spicy filling of mashed potato.

SERVES: 4   V

Pastry
1 tablespoon vegetable oil
4 oz (115 g) strong white plain flour
   or 4 sheets filo pastry

Flour and Water Paste
1 tablespoon plain flour

Filling
$\frac{1}{2}$ lb mashed potato
1 tablespoon cashew nuts, chopped

1 teaspoon coconut milk powder
$\frac{1}{2}$–2 green chilli, chopped
1 tablespoon fresh coriander, chopped
1 teaspoon brown sugar

Spices (roasted)
1 teaspoon mustard seeds
1 teaspoon cummin seeds

1 Mix the oil and flour and enough water to make a dough which when mixed does not stick to the bowl. Leave to stand for about one hour.

2 At the same time make a flour and water paste (to stick the samosas together).

3 Mix the (cold) filling ingredients together with the **spices**.

4 Divide pastry into two. Roll each piece, or cut the file pastry into two thin 12 in (30 cm) squares. The thinner you can get the pastry, the crispier will be your samosas. Cut in half diagonally, then trim tips off as in diagram 1. Fold over as shown in diagrams 2, 3 and 4. Stick sides together with flour and water paste to form a pouch.

5 Stuff with filling. Fold over the top and secure with flour and water paste.

6 Deep fry at 375°F/190°C for 8 minutes.

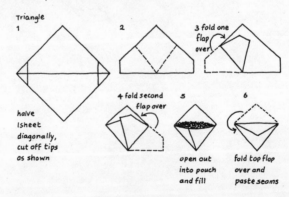

74

CHAPTER FIVE

Vegetable Curries

This chapter is the longest in the book. I have called it 'vegetable curries' and I feel this needs a brief explanation.

Firstly, all the recipes in this chapter are vegan, which means that dairy produce and eggs are excluded.

Secondly, the recipes are grouped together in vegetable types. The chapter starts with leaf vegetables. A selection of fruit and root vegetables comes next. This is followed by a selection of potato recipes, and the chapter ends with a group of interesting recipes which involve such delights as bean sprouts and noodles. Within these loose categories I have incorporated secondary ingredients which add interest to both taste and texture, such as nuts, wheat, currants and coconut. The combination of ingredients has also been chosen to give good colour contrasts that create visual appeal in the individual dishes.

The final point about these recipes in particular is that, although I have specified the main and secondary ingredients in each recipe, there is no reason at all why you should not change these ingredients to those of your own choice whilst following the basic method and spicing. In that way you will be able to extend the range of options in the chapter by an unlimited amount.

Sabzi Rawash

Spinach with Rhubarb

Although one rarely encounters rhubarb in India it is very popular in Afghanistan. So is spinach. And this dish brings the two unexpectedly together in a delicious savoury combination, proving that with a little imagination a vegetarian's life is never dull!

SERVES: 4   V

1½ lb (675 g) spinach leaves and tender stalks, weighed after trimming
2 stalks rhubarb
4 tablespoons vegetable oil
2 teaspoons garlic purée
2 teaspoons onion purée
1 tablespoon cummin seeds
1 tablespoon sugar

2 tablespoons chopped fresh coriander leaves
chilli powder
aromatic salt to taste

Spices
1 teaspoon cummin seeds
½ teaspoon wild onion seeds

1 Wash the spinach several times to remove grit and soil. Shake off excess water then coarsely chop it up, including the tender parts of the stalks.

2 Wash the rhubarb and cut it into about ½ inch (1·25 cm) pieces.

3 Start to boil up about 2 pints (1·2 litres) water in a 4 pint (2·25 litre) saucepan.

4 Heat the oil in a *karahi* or wok. Stir-fry the garlic and onion purées for up to 3 minutes. Add the **spices** and continue stir-frying for 2 more minutes.

5 Add about ½ cup of water then, when it starts to simmer, add the rhubarb. Simmer for about 10 minutes, stirring occasionally, and if it starts to dry up add a little more water.

6 Meanwhile, when the saucepan of water (stage 3) starts to boil, put in the spinach and simmer for about 10 minutes.

7 Strain the spinach and add it, hot, to the karahi.

8 Stir-fry for about 2 or 3 more minutes, then add the cummin seed, sugar, fresh coriander, chilli powder and salt to taste.

9 Serve when ready.

Ganthgobi Ke Sag

Kohlrabi and Indian Leaves

I obtained this recipe from a cook in Kashmir. There, on the stunning Srinagar lakes, I once spent a week on one of the exquisite sandalwood houseboats. Each boat is like a miniature floating hotel and comes complete with its own cook. This was one of our cook's recipes.

The principal vegetable is kohlrabi or knol-kohl, a bulbous root vegetable resembling a turnip with lush green leaves. It is a hardy vegetable and thrives in mountainous districts such as Kashmir. Only the leaves are used in this dish, augmented with any other green leaves that are to hand, such as spinach, green cabbage and radish leaves. The kohlrabi roots can be used in salads or other cooking, such as the recipe on page 86.

SERVES: 4   V

$1\frac{1}{2}$ lb (675 g) green vegetable leaves, of which all or most should be kohlrabi, weighed after discarding unwanted matter
6 tablespoons mustard or sesame oil
$\frac{1}{8}$ teaspoon asafoetida
2 tablespoons black mustard seeds
2–4 cloves garlic, cut into thin julienne strips

8 oz (225 g) onion, cut into thin julienne strips
2 inch (5 cm) cube fresh ginger, cut into thin julienne strips
dry red chillies to taste, coarsely chopped (optional)
1 tablespoon brown sugar
salt to taste

1 Discard unwanted matter from the kohlrabi leaves, but use the soft parts of the stalks. Wash, drain and chop coarsely.

2 Boil all the greens for 10 minutes, then drain.

3 During stage 2, heat the oil in a *karahi* or wok. Stir-fry the asafoetida, mustard seeds and garlic for 1 minute. Add the onion and ginger and continue to stir-fry for 2 more minutes. Add a half cup of water, the optional chillies and the sugar, and bring to a simmer.

4 Add the drained greens, and stir-fry until the mixture is simmering again. Add salt to taste, then serve.

Ghaw Be Thot

Burmese Cabbage

This is a very light, crisp vegetable dish from Burma, which makes the most of white cabbage and Chinese leaves. Cooking time is minimal, with a short blanch and a stir-fry which gives the vegetables a glistening appearance. The turmeric gives a golden colour and the greens and reds of the peppers give the whole dish tremendous visual appeal.

SERVES: 4   V

1 lb (450 g) white cabbage
8 oz (225 g) Chinese leaves
4 tablespoons sunflower or vegetable oil
2–4 teaspoons garlic purée
3 teaspoons sesame seeds
1 teaspoon turmeric
4–6 spring onions, cut into thin rings including leaves

$\frac{1}{4}$–$\frac{1}{2}$ red capsicum pepper, cut into strips
1–4 fresh green chillies, chopped
salt to taste

Garnish
1 tablespoon finely chopped fresh coriander leaves

1 Chop the cabbage and Chinese leaves into thinnish strips, discarding stalky pieces. Blanch in boiling water, then drain.

2 During stage 1, heat the oil in a *karahi* or wok. Stir-fry the garlic, sesame seeds and turmeric for 1 minute. Add the spring onions, red pepper and chillies and stir-fry for 5 minutes.

3 Add the drained vegetables, stir-frying until simmering. The mixture should be neither too dry nor too wet, but add a little water if needed. Add salt to taste. Garnish with the coriander and serve piping hot.

Mallung

Broccoli in Courgette and Coconut

From the pearl-shaped beautiful island of Sri Lanka comes the *mallung*. It is a curry with a rich coconut sauce, using vegetables to hand. I have chosen to use broccoli and courgettes. The combination of colours and textures of these two suits the dish well, but you can use any vegetables of your choice. You must, however, use a fresh coconut; only then will you get the fresh tastes that the dish deserves.

SERVES: 4   V

1 fresh coconut (see stage 1)
1 oz (25 g) coconut milk powder
¾ lb (350 g) broccoli, weighed after
   trimming
¾ lb (350 g) courgettes, weighed after
   trimming
3 tablespoons mustard or coconut oil
8 oz (225 g) onion, thinly sliced
2–6 fresh green chillies, chopped
   (optional)

salt to taste
½ teaspoon (about ¼ g) saffron
2 tablespoons fresh whole coriander
   leaves, stalks removed

Spices
1 tablespoon black mustard seeds
6–10 fresh or dried curry leaves (if
   available)

1 Prepare the coconut (see page 37), keeping the water aside and finely grating the flesh of one half only. (Use the remainder for another recipe.)

2 Mix the coconut milk powder with enough water to make a runny paste.

3 Trim leaves and excess stalks off the broccoli and top and tail the courgettes, then wash them both.

4 Cut the broccoli into small florets and slice the courgettes into discs about ⅓ inch (8 mm) thick.

5 Bring to the boil 2 pans of water. Boil the courgettes for 8–10 minutes and the broccoli for 10–12 minutes. Drain and combine them.

6 Meanwhile, heat the oil in a *karahi* or wok. Stir-fry the **spices** for 1 minute. Add the onion and the optional chillies and stir-fry for about 10 minutes.

7 Add in the coconut water, the shredded coconut flesh and the drained vegetables. Stir-fry until sizzling, then add the coconut milk paste. You should now have a relatively runny creamy sauce. (It may need a little water to achieve this.) Add salt to taste.

8 Add the saffron and fresh coriander leaves, and, when hot, serve at once.

Thoran or Thovaran

Carrot, Cabbage and Coconut

The texture of this dish is very light, as is the spicing. The cabbage is shredded, the carrot grated and the coconut (which really must be fresh) is scraped. It is a southern Indian favourite, where it is normally served hot as one dish of a meal served on a banana leaf. I have also found that it makes an excellent cold dish, as a starter or snack. This dish is also called *porial* in Tamil, *koora* in Andrah Pradesh and *palya* in Mysore.

SERVES: 4   V

4 tablespoons polished split urid dhal
1 fresh coconut, using all its water
   and half its flesh (see page 37 for
   preparation)
2 oz (50 g) coconut milk powder
12 oz (350 g) white cabbage, shredded
6 tablespoons mustard oil
2 tablespoons mustard seeds

12 oz (350 g) carrot, grated
salt to taste

Spices
2 teaspoon cummin seeds
3 or 4 dried red chillies
½ teaspoon turmeric

1 Soak the urid dhal for up to 6 hours in ample water. Drain.

2 Roast the **spices** for a minute or so (see page 24).

3 When cool, grind them finely with the fresh coconut water and flesh. Add the coconut milk powder and enough water to make it into a paste.

4 Blanch the shredded cabbage for no more than 5 minutes. Drain.

5 During stage 4, heat the oil in a *karahi* or wok and stir-fry the mustard seeds and urid dhal for 2–3 minutes.

6 Add the spice and coconut paste and stir-fry until simmering.

7 Then add the cabbage and carrot. As soon as it is hot, add salt to taste and serve.

Kurass Ke Phul Gobhi Masala

Celery and Cauliflower Dry Curry

The recipe for this curry comes from eastern India, an area largely ignored by tourists but as full of life, interesting sights and gastronomic delights as anywhere else in India. The combination of celery and cauliflower works very well, the one being complementary to the other. But do feel free to use your own choice of vegetables – the spice mixture (masala) works well with anything.

SERVES: 4   V

½ lb (225 g) celery
1 lb (450 g) cauliflower florets,
   weighed after preparation
4–6 tablespoons vegetable oil
2–4 teaspoons garlic purée
2 teaspoons ginger purée
4–6 fresh tomatoes, chopped
aromatic salt to taste

Spices
2 teaspoons cummin seeds
1 teaspoon black mustard seeds
1 teaspoon coriander seeds
1 teaspoon turmeric
½–1 teaspoon chilli powder

1 Cut the celery into 1 inch (2·5 cm) pieces after cleaning.

2 Cut the cauliflower into small florets.

3 Boil the celery for about 5 minutes and the cauliflower for 10–15 minutes. Drain them both.

4 During stage 3, heat the oil in a *karahi* or wok. Stir-fry the **spices** for about 1 minute. Add the garlic and ginger and stir-fry for a further minute.

5 Add the tomatoes and, when sizzling and soft, add the celery and cauliflower and stir-fry, mixing well. It will be quite dry, which is intentional, but add a little water to prevent burning while it heats up. Add salt to taste and serve at once. This dish can be cooled and reheated, or frozen, but it will not be as crisp.

Sambal Bendi

Fried Okra, Malaysian Style

Malaya is a peninsula in the Far East thronging with an energetic population from a number of widely different cultural backgrounds, one of which is India.

This stir-fry dish makes the most of okra and the spices it is cooked with. The Indian version is similar and is called *bindi bhajee*.

SERVES: 4   V

1½ lb (675 g) okra
4 tablespoons sunflower or sesame oil
2 oz (50 g) onion, finely chopped
2 cloves garlic, finely chopped
dash Worcestershire sauce
aromatic salt to taste
sugar to taste
1 tablespoon fresh coriander, chopped

Spices
1 teaspoon ground cummin
½ teaspoon turmeric
½ teaspoon chilli powder

1 Wash the okra, leaving them whole until stage 3.

2 Heat the oil in a *karahi* or wok. Stir-fry the onion and garlic for 2–3 minutes. Add the spices and the Worcestershire sauce and continue to stir-fry for a further 2–3 minutes.

3 During stage 2 cut off and discard the okra stalks then cut the flesh into pieces about 1 inch (2·5 cm) long. Place them straight away into the *karahi* and stir-fry for between 5 and 8 minutes, depending on the crispness you want. Sprinkle a little water into the *karahi* as needed during the stir-fry to prevent sticking.

4 Add salt and sugar to taste and the fresh coriander, and after a quick brisk final stir-fry, serve at once.

Thakkali Bendakka

Cherry Tomatoes and Okra Curry

From Sri Lanka comes this colourful tasty curry. Choose the okra carefully: some can be very scaly. Usually, but not always, small ones are tenderest.

There is only one way to cook okra, in my view, and that is to stir-fry them. The application of water by boiling, or even steaming, causes the okra to go very sticky and sappy. The dish should be served as soon as it is cooked; whilst it does freeze, it will never be as crisp or fresh.

SERVES: 4   V

1¼ lb (550 g) okra (lady's fingers)
8 oz (225 g) cherry tomatoes
6 tablespoons sesame or sunflower oil
2–6 cloves garlic, thinly sliced
2 inch (5 cm) cube fresh ginger, finely sliced
4 oz (110 g) onion, finely chopped
salt to taste

Spices
1 teaspoon ground cummin
1 teaspoon cummin seeds
1 teaspoon ground coriander
½ teaspoon paprika
½ teaspoon turmeric
¼ teaspoon mango powder
⅛ teaspoon asafoetida

1 Mix the **spices** with enough water to make a thickish paste.

2 Wash and dry the okra and set them aside.

3 Wash the tomatoes after removing the stalks.

4 Heat the oil in a *karahi* or wok. Stir-fry the garlic and ginger for about 2 minutes. Add the onion and the spice paste and continue to stir-fry for 5 minutes or so.

5 During this time (and, to prevent them going sappy, no earlier), cut the stalks off the okra. You can slice the okra into discs, but I prefer to keep them whole.

6 Add them to the *karahi* with the tomatoes and briskly stir-fry for 5 minutes. They will be sealed by then, at which time you can add a little water to create a gravy. Add salt to taste and, as soon as the curry is hot, serve.

Imasha or Mahasha

Stuffed Tomatoes

This dish originates from the Middle East, where a similarly named dish exists today. It probably made its way to Cochin in southern India with the first Christians who landed in the area with St Thomas the Apostle in the first century AD.

Imasha is basically stuffed vegetables. You can stuff any vegetable – potato, onion, capsicum pepper, aubergine, courgette, etc. In this recipe I use good firm beefsteak tomatoes.

MAKES: 8 *imasha*   **V**

4 firm beefsteak or marmande tomatoes, about 3½ inches (9 cm) across
1 cupful fresh coriander leaves, with stalks
vegetable oil for deep frying
2 oz (50 g) thawed frozen or cooked fresh peas
1 tablespoon curry paste

0–4 fresh green chillies (optional)
8 oz (225 g) mashed potato
aromatic salt to taste

Spices
2 teaspoons cummin seeds
1 teaspoon mustard seeds
1 teaspoon garlic powder
½ teaspoon mango powder

1 Halve the tomatoes and, without making a hole in the case, carefully scoop out and reserve the seeds and centre pulp.

2 Heat the deep-fryer to 375°F/190°C and deep-fry the fresh coriander for a few seconds. It will whoosh and cook fast. Drain, then crumble it up.

3 Mix the peas, **spices,** curry paste, optional chillies, tomato pulp and the crumbled fried coriander leaves with the mashed potato. Add salt to taste. The mixture should be soft and mouldable.

4 Preheat the oven to 325°F/160°C/Gas 3. Spoon the potato mixture into the tomatoes and place them on a sheet of foil on an oven tray. Bake for 15–20 minutes. Serve hot or cold.

Sabzi Haleem

Diced Root Vegetables with Whole Wheat

In central India is the former state of Hyderabad, once the home of one of the richest maharajas, and still the home of a large Moslem community. One of their unique dishes is ground meat with whole wheat – *haleem*. I have adapted this to make a vegetarian version. Instead of meat I am using mashed red sweet potato (American yam) plus celeriac, Jerusalem artichoke, parsnip and carrot.

SERVES: 4   V

2 oz (50 g) whole wheat
12 oz (350 g) red sweet potato
  (American yam)
1 bulb celeriac
2 or 3 Jerusalem artichokes
1 medium-sized parsnip
2 medium-sized carrots
4 tablespoons vegetable oil
2 teaspoons garlic purée
2 teaspoons ginger purée

4 oz (110 g) onion, chopped
¼ pint (150 ml) akhni stock or water
2 tablespoons garam masala
aromatic salt to taste

Spices
2 teaspoons ground coriander
2 teaspoons ground cummin
2 teaspoons curry powder (page 25)

1 Soak the wheat in ample water overnight. Prior to cooking, rinse several times and drain. Boil for about 20 minutes, then drain.

2 Peel the sweet potato and boil it, then mash as for ordinary potatoes.

3 Quarter the celeriac, and peel it and dice into ¼ inch cubes. Do the same with the Jerusalem artichokes, parsnip and carrots.

4 Boil these together until tender but not overcooked. (Test after 10 minutes.)

5 During stage 4, heat the oil in a *karahi* or wok. Stir-fry the garlic and ginger for 2 minutes. Add the **spices** and continue for 2 more minutes, then add the onions and stir-fry for about 5 minutes.

6 Add the akhni stock or water and the wheat and simmer for about 10 minutes, until the liquid is reduced by about half.

7 Add the roots and tubers. When simmering, add the mashed yam and garam masala and mix together well. Add salt to taste.

8 The mixture will now be the texture of mashed potato and, when hot, it is ready to serve.

Sabzi Durbar

Special Vegetable Curry

A *durbar* is the levee or assembly of an Indian ruler's court. At the time of the Raj it was the British Viceroy who headed the durbars, and these were often celebrated with a procession of great magnificence and a banquet, for which dishes of equal splendour were invented. This recipe, which I found in a very old cookery book, could well have been one of them.

SERVES: 4   V

2–3 medium-sized carrots
6 inch (15 cm) piece mooli (white
   radish) or 1 kohlrabi bulb
6–8 spinach leaves
6 oz (175 g) peas, fresh or thawed
   frozen
6 oz (175 g) sweetcorn, fresh or
   thawed frozen
2 oz (50 g) redcurrants (about
   ½ cupful)
1 firm avocado pear
1 firm mango

6 tablespoons vegetable oil
2–4 cloves garlic
1 tablespoon fresh coriander leaves
salt to taste

Spices
1 teaspoon ground cummin
1 teaspoon sesame seeds
½ teaspoon wild onion seeds
½ teaspoon aniseeds
½ teaspoon mustard seeds

1 Dice the carrot and mooli or kohlrabi into small cubes of about ¼ inch (6 mm), keeping the vegetables separate. Clean and remove the stalks from the spinach and cut the leaves into ½ inch (1·25 cm) shreds.

2 Boil the mooli or kohlrabi for about 5 minutes and drain. Use the same water to boil the carrots for the same time, then drain. In a separate saucepan, boil the spinach for 5 minutes and drain. Fresh peas and sweetcorn will also require a similar boil, but if using frozen ones (acceptable for this recipe) simply thaw them by immersing in hot water. Drain when required.

3 Remove the stalks and wash the redcurrants. Halve and stone the avocado; scoop out the flesh and dice it into ¼ inch (6 mm) cubes. Do the same with the mango.

4 Heat the oil in a *karahi* or wok and stir-fry the **spices** for 1 minute. Add the garlic and continue to stir-fry for a further minute.

5 All that remains to do is to stir-fry the vegetables until they are hot, starting with the firmest: the carrot and radish first, next the peas and sweetcorn and, when they are hot, the spinach and the fresh coriander. Stir-fry gently and add salt to taste at this stage.

6 Finally and carefully, add the soft items: the redcurrants, mango and avocado. Slowly stir-fry, preventing the soft items from breaking up and spoiling the appearance of the dish. When hot, serve at once.

Kuah La Da

Peppery Vegetable Curry

This recipe hails from Malaysia. I obtained it from a very entertaining cookery course given by Terry Chan, at Ken Lo's Kitchen. Terry is a well-known expert on the food of his own country, Malaya, and this recipe, using aubergine, courgette, cabbage and spices, is one of his best.

SERVES: 4   V

1 large aubergine
4 courgettes
2 large green cabbage leaves
3 tablespoons vegetable oil
1 tablespoon tamarind purée
salt and sugar to taste

Spice Paste
2–4 cloves garlic

8 oz (225 g) onion, chopped
1 inch (2·5 cm) cube fresh ginger or
* galingale*
4–6 candlenuts (kemeri) or
* macadamia or cashew nuts*
2 dried red chillies
1 teaspoon turmeric
1 teaspoon ground black pepper

1 Put the **spice paste** ingredients into a food processor or blender and grind until smooth, using minimal water as needed.

2 Wash all the vegetables. Cut the top off the aubergine and dice it into pieces about 1 inch (2·5 cm) square. Top and tail the courgettes and slice them. Place both these in ample cold water to prevent discolouring. Coarsely cut up the cabbage leaves, removing any inedible stalks etc.

3 Heat the oil in a *karahi* or wok. Stir-fry the **spice paste** for about 4 minutes. Add the tamarind purée and about 1 pint (600 ml) water. Bring to the boil and add the vegetables.

4 Simmer for about 5 minutes, then add salt and sugar to taste. Serve with a rice or noodle dish.

Chyau

Nepali Mushroom

When I obtained this recipe from a Nepalese chef from the celebrated Annapurna Hotel in Kathmandu, he impressed upon me that it was regarded by the Nepalese as a dish with certain properties. He kept calling it his magic mushroom recipe, and what he was telling me was that it was a special mushroom grown in summer high up in the Himalayan mountains. And its properties, he assured me, were very special indeed. They were aphrodisiac. I must say, I greatly enjoyed the dish he cooked.

Unfortunately we cannot obtain this particular species of mushroom in the West, so I cannot promise the same properties when you cook it at home. But despite that, it is no less delicious using any type of mushroom. And who knows . . .?

SERVES: 4   V

1 lb (450 g) mushrooms
1 teaspoon fenugreek seeds
2 tablespoons vegetable oil
4 oz (110 g) onion, finely chopped
2–4 cloves garlic, finely chopped

1 inch (2·5 cm) cube fresh ginger,
  finely chopped
½ teaspoon turmeric
1 teaspoon chilli powder (optional)
aromatic salt to taste

1 Clean the mushrooms as necessary.

2 Soak the fenugreek seeds in ample water for a couple of hours, then drain.

3 Heat the oil in a *karahi* or wok and stir-fry the soaked fenugreek seeds for a minute. Add the onion, garlic and ginger and stir-fry for 3–4 minutes. Add the turmeric and optional chilli powder and continue to fry for a further minute.

4 Add enough water to make the stir-fry into a medium-thickness paste.

5 When it is simmering add salt to taste, then add the mushrooms. Serve as soon as they are hot.

Hathichowk Chettinad

Stir-Fry Artichoke

In the state of Tamil Nadu in southern India there is a community called the Chettiyars, who were amongst the earliest settlers in the area. They are avid meat eaters and the original recipe for this stir-fry dish uses chicken.

However, as with all recipes, it is quite easy to convert it to vegetarian. For the principal ingredient, choose a tasty fleshy vegetable. Particularly suitable is Jerusalem artichoke, which is easy to cook (like a potato), is robust enough to stir-fry and has a distinctive flavour.

SERVES: 4   V

1½ lb (675 g) Jerusalem artichokes	*Spices*
6 tablespoons mustard oil	1 tablespoon black mustard seeds
8 oz (225 g) onion, finely sliced	1 teaspoon turmeric
2–6 fresh red or green chillies,	1 teaspoon paprika
chopped (optional)	½ teaspoon whole aniseeds
1 tablespoon curry paste	¼ teaspoon whole lovage seeds
aromatic salt to taste	
2 oz (50 g) cashew nuts, deep-fried	
1 tablespoon fresh coriander, chopped	

1 Trim and peel the artichokes and dice into about 1 inch (2·5 cm) cubes. Boil them until tender, then drain.

2 Heat the oil in a *karahi* or wok. Stir-fry the **spices** for 1 minute; add the onion and optional chillies and continue stir-frying for about 5 more minutes. Add the curry paste and the cooked and drained artichokes and get them sizzling as they stir-fry. Add sprinklings of water to prevent the ingredients from sticking and stir-fry for about 5 minutes. Add salt to taste. Add the cashew nuts and fresh coriander and, when these are hot, serve at once.

Pakari

Pineapple, Peanut and Coconut Curry

Sweetness is the theme in this Indonesian recipe. Pineapple is added to a creamy coconut-based sauce, which itself is lightly spiced and enhanced with peanuts.

SERVES: 4   V

1 pineapple
2 oz (50 g) desiccated coconut
½ fresh coconut and its water or 2 oz
  (50 g) coconut milk powder
4 tablespoons vegetable or coconut oil
4 oz (110 g) raw peanuts
2–4 cloves garlic, finely chopped
4 oz (110 g) onion, finely chopped
aromatic salt to taste

Spices
2 teaspoons ground coriander
1 teaspoon ground cummin
½ teaspoon ground cassia bark or
  cinnamon
½ teaspoon turmeric
½ teaspoon ground black pepper
1 tablespoon sugar (optional)

1 Prepare the pineapple, removing the outer husks and 'eyes'. Halve it and, avoiding the pithy centre core, cut the flesh into about 1 inch (2·5 cm) cubes. Set aside.

2 Put the desiccated coconut under the grill and apply medium heat until it is buff coloured. Allow to cool.

3 Use either fresh coconut flesh ground with its own water or coconut milk powder mixed with water to obtain a runny paste.

4 Heat the oil in a *karahi* or wok and stir-fry the peanuts for a couple of minutes. Drain them and set aside.

5 Reheat the same oil in the *kahari* and stir-fry the garlic for 1 minute. Add the onion and continue to fry for a further 3–4 minutes. Add **spices** and stir-fry for another 2–3 minutes.

6 Now add the coconut paste and briskly stir-fry until it starts to stick to the pan.

7 At once add enough water to make the mixture into a medium-thickness purée. Add the pineapple chunks and bring to a simmer. Add salt to taste.

8 Adjust the thickness of the dish by adding a little more water if required, then add the peanuts. When hot, serve garnished with the toasted desiccated coconut. Alternatively, garnish with shreds of raw fresh coconut.

Theeval Kootoo

Potato and Peas in a Hot and Sour Sauce

The Tamils, who live in Sri Lanka and South India, adore the taste combination of hot, sour and coconut, which they create by liberally using chilli, tamarind and fresh coconut – as in this recipe.

SERVES: 4   V

1 fresh coconut or 2 oz (50 g)
  desiccated coconut and 2 oz (50 g)
  coconut milk powder
1 lb (450 g) potatoes (tiny new ones
  are best)
6 tablespoons coconut or vegetable oil
2–6 cloves garlic, thinly sliced
2–4 inch (5–10 cm) cube fresh ginger,
  thinly sliced
8 oz (225 g) onion, thinly sliced
4 oz (110 g) cooked fresh or thawed
  frozen peas
6–8 fresh green or red chillies,
  chopped

1–2 tablespoons tamarind purée
salt to taste
fresh coriander leaves for garnish

Spices 1
1 teaspoon ground coriander
1 teaspoon garam masala
1 teaspoon turmeric

Spices 2
1 teaspoon cummin seeds
1 teaspoon black mustard seeds
8–10 curry leaves, fresh or dried

1 Prepare the coconut (see page 37). Reserve the water for use in stage 4. Grate the flesh of about half the coconut, then grill it for about 1 minute. If using desiccated coconut, grill it for the same time and make a thin paste of the coconut milk powder by adding ordinary water.

2 Small new potatoes need scrubbing, but not peeling. Boil until just tender, rinse and drain, keeping them hot.

3 During stage 2, heat the oil in a *karahi* or wok. Stir-fry **spices 1** for 1 minute, then the garlic for 1 minute; add the ginger and stir-fry for a minute, then the onion and continue for about 2 minutes. Finally add **spices 2** and stir-fry them in for another minute.

4 Add enough coconut water (and/or ordinary water) to make a runny gravy, then put in the potatoes, peas, chillies and tamarind purée.

5 Simmer for about 10 minutes, adding more water as it reduces. Add salt to taste. Garnish with fresh coriander leaves and serve.

Badami Dum

Potato Stuffed with Almonds Topped with a Spicy Gravy

As traditional Indian cooking has evolved without the use of ovens, the technique of baking is rare. This recipe was created by one of India's most innovative chefs, my great friend and culinary mentor Satish Arora, Director of cooking for the *Taj Group of Hotels* based in Bombay. His combination of baked potato, nut stuffing and spicy gravy makes this a meal in its own right. For a delightful non-vegan variation, mix the nut and garam masala with several tablespoons of thick Greek yoghurt and/or grated Cheddar cheese.

SERVES: 4   [V]

*4 large baking potatoes, scrubbed but
  not peeled*
vegetable ghee (not melted)
*2 or 3 tablespoons finely chopped fresh
  coriander leaves*

The Stuffing
*$3\frac{1}{2}$ oz (100 g) almonds, coarsely
  chopped*
2 tablespoons garam masala
vegetable ghee

The Gravy
*4 portions (1 'mould') curry masala
  gravy (page 31)*

1   Preheat the oven to 350°F/180°C/Gas 4.

2   Smear each potato with ghee and scatter the fresh coriander all over. Wrap in foil and place on an oven tray in the oven. Bake for about 1 hour.

3   During this time, prepare the stuffing and the gravy.

4   For the stuffing, simply mix the chopped almonds with the garam masala and a little ghee. Set aside.

5   At the end of the hour, test that the potatoes are cooked by poking into the centre with a small knife. It should slide through without resistance. If there is a little uncooked portion in the centre, return to the oven.

6   When cooked, unwrap the potatoes from the foil. Slit along the long side to the mid point. Carefully scoop out some potato (use it in another recipe) and replace it with the stuffing. Return the potatoes to the oven for 10 more minutes.

7   Gently heat the gravy and pour it over the potatoes. Serve as a snack or as an accompaniment to a main meal.

Methi Aloo Burta

Potato Fry with Fenugreek

The slightly bitter and intensely savoury flavour of this stir-fry dish is particularly typical of the Punjab area of India and neighbouring Pakistan. Fresh fenugreek leaves are best if you can get them (easy if you have an Indo-Pakistan community near you), but dried leaves are almost as good.

SERVES: 4   V

1 lb (450 g) potatoes
3 tablespoons vegetable oil
1 red pepper, finely chopped
2–4 fresh green chillies, finely
 chopped (optional)
4 tablespoons chopped fresh coriander
 leaves
6 oz (175 g) fresh fenugreek leaves,
 stalks removed and chopped or *2*
 tablespoons dried funugreek leaves
aromatic salt to taste

Spices
2 tablespoons dried coriander seeds,
 roasted and crushed
1 teaspoon cummin seeds
1 teaspoon mango powder
½ teaspoon turmeric
½ teaspoon ground fenugreek seeds
⅛ teaspoon asafoetida

1 Peel the potatoes, dice them into 1½ inch (3·75 cm) cubes and boil until soft (15 to 20 minutes). Do not overcook.

2 During this time, heat the oil in a *karahi* or wok and stir-fry the **spices** for about 1 minute. Add the red pepper and the (optional) fresh green chillies and stir-fry for about 3 minutes.

3 Add about a cupful of water and bring to a simmer. Add the fresh coriander and fresh or dried fenugreek leaves. Simmer for about 10 minutes. Add salt to taste.

4 By now the potatoes should be ready. Drain and add them to the *karahi*. Toss to ensure everything is well mixed, then serve.

Rataloo Katki

Sweet Potato and Mango

This recipe comes from the Sindh area of Pakistan. Its use of sweet potato and fresh mango gives a unique combination of sweet and sour which the light spicing enhances enormously.

SERVES: 4   V

1 lb (450 g) white sweet potato
6 tablespoons sesame or sunflower oil
4 oz (110 g) onion, finely chopped
1 large firm mango
aromatic salt to taste
2–3 tablespoons finely chopped fresh
   coriander leaves

Spices
2 teaspoons cummin seeds
2–4 dried red chillies
1 teaspoon black mustard seeds
1 teaspoon mango powder
½ teaspoon ground green cardamom

1 Scrub the sweet potatoes but do not peel them. Dice them into 1½ inch (3·75 cm) cubes.

2 Heat the oil in a *karahi* or wok. Stir-fry the **spices** for 1 minute, then add the onion and continue for about 5 more minutes.

3 Add the potato cubes and stir-fry for about 10 minutes.

4 During stage 3, cut open the mango and cut away the flesh from the skin and stone. If it is very soft, scoop it out; if firm, use a knife and dice it into ¼ inch (6 mm) pieces.

5 Add the mango to the stir-fry with, if it is sticking, a splash of water. Keep on stir-frying for another 5 minutes or so. Add salt to taste.

6 Serve hot, garnished with the fresh coriander leaves.

Note: If you can obtain it, the Indian *arbi* (also called *taro* or *dasheen*) can be used instead of sweet potato to produce a truly authentic version of this dish. It should be peeled at stage 1.

Sabzi Sali Patia

Sweet Potato, Beetroot and Tomato in a Sweet and Savoury Gravy

The combinaton of sweet and savoury is particularly relished by the Parsee community of Bombay, and their dish Patia exemplifies this particularly well. In this version the sweetness is enhanced with sweet potato.

The beetroot and tomato give the dish a gorgeous colour. The garnish of *sali* potato straws adds a crunchy texture and an attractive appearance to the dish.

SERVES: 4   V

1 lb (450 g) red sweet potatoes
  (American yam)
1 medium-sized cooked beetroot
6 red tomatoes or 15 cherry tomatoes
3 tablespoons vegetable oil
2 tablespoons garlic purée
2 tablespoons ginger purée
8 oz (225 g) onion purée
6 fl oz (175 ml) akhni stock or water
1 tablespoon brown sugar

1 tablespoon tamarind purée or 1
  tablespoon lemon juice
aromatic salt to taste
garnish of sali potato straws

Spices
2 teaspoons tandoori masala
2 teaspoons white sesame seeds
1 teaspoon aniseed
1 teaspoon paprika
1 teaspoon cummin seeds

1 Make a thick paste of the **spices** using a little water, and set aside.

2 Scrub the red sweet potatoes but do not peel them. Dice them into 1½ inch (3·75 cm) cubes.

3 Blanch them in boiling water for 2–3 minutes. Drain and set aside.

4 Peel the beetroot and cut it into julienne strips (matchsticks).

5 Blanch and peel the tomatoes, then quarter them. If using cherry tomatoes, wash them and add them whole in stage 8 (below).

6 Heat the oil in a *karahi* or wok. Stir-fry the garlic, ginger and onion purées for about 5 minutes, then add the spice paste. Stir-fry for a further 3–4 minutes.

7 Add the akhni stock or water and, when simmering, add the sweet potato cubes.

8 Simmer for about 5 minutes, then add the beetroot, tomatoes, sugar and tamarind purée or lemon juice. Stir well and add salt to taste.

9 Serve hot, garnished with the sali.

Peeteepeepowk Onon

Burmese Bean Sprouts in Coconut Milk

Bean sprouts are nearly always associated with Chinese food. In fact bean sprouts, sometimes called bean shoots, are widely encountered in Indo-Chinese, Thai and Burmese food. This Burmese recipe achieves a remarkable combination of tastes, textures and colour. Do not blanch the sprouts. Use absolutely fresh crisp white sprouts and stir-fry them into the 'sauce' immediately prior to serving. The coconut and turmeric combine to make a lovely pale yellow colour, enhancing the whiteness of the bean sprouts. A green garnish makes the most of this crispy crunchy dish.

SERVES: 4   V

1 lb (450 g) bean sprouts
6–10 spring onions, including leaves
2 tablespoons vegetable oil
2–4 cloves garlic, finely chopped
2 inch (5 cm) cube fresh ginger, finely
* chopped*

½ teaspoon turmeric
2 oz (50 g) coconut milk powder
salt to taste
green garnish of fresh coriander leaves
* and/or parsley and/or spring onion*
* leaves*

1 Wash and drain the bean sprouts.

2 Chop the spring onions in thin slices (thicker for the leaves). Reserve a sprinkling of leaves for garnishing.

3 Heat the oil in a *karahi* or wok. Stir-fry the garlic for 1 minute, add the ginger and continue for another minute, then add the spring onions and stir-fry for a further 2–3 minutes. Add the turmeric and stir-fry for a final minute.

4 Mix the coconut milk powder with enough water to obtain a thin cream consistency, then add it to the *karahi*.

5 When simmering, add the bean sprouts. Stir-fry until hot. The mixture should not be dry so add a little water if needed. Season, garnish with coriander and/or parsley and/or spring onion leaves and serve immediately.

Peeteepeepowk Net Shwe   V

Bean Sprouts with Deep-Fried Golden Tofu

8 oz (225 g) deep-fried tofu or
* paneer (page 36)*

Add the finished hot tofu or paneer to *Peeteepeepowk Onon* prior to serving.

Mee Krob

◆

Crisp-Fried Thread Noodles with Sauce

The traditional *mee krob* is a Thai classic. It normally includes seafood and meat, but in this version it is the noodles themselves which feature, united with a spicy sweet-and-sour sauce. It makes an excellent crunchy, tasty garnish or side dish.

SERVES: 4   V

*6 tablespoons sunflower or other light
  oil
2oz (50g) brown sugar
soy sauce to taste
4fl oz (100ml) vinegar (any type)
4 teaspoons garlic purée*

*4oz (110g) spring onion leaves and
  bulbs, finely chopped
2 teaspoons chilli powder (optional)
vegetable oil for deep-frying
9oz (250g) bean thread vermicelli
  noodles*

1 Heat the sunflower oil in a *karahi* or wok. Carefully add the sugar, soy sauce and vinegar to the *karahi* (it will splutter if the oil is too hot), then increase the heat whilst stir-frying for about 5 minutes.

2 Add the garlic purée, chopped spring onions and optional chilli powder and stir-fry for a further 2 minutes. You should now have a fairly glutinous syrupy texture. Take off the heat.

3 Heat the deep-fryer to 375°F/190°C. Split the noodles into 3 or 4 bundles. Carefully put the first bundle into the deep-fryer. It will whoosh up and swell. Once the sizzling stops (in less than a minute), remove it and drain. Cook the remaining noodles in the same way.

4 Prior to serving, reheat the sauce in the *karahi* or wok. Place the noodles in bit by bit and, without breaking them up, try to get the sauce to cover as much of the noodles as possible. Alternatively pour the sauce over the noodles.

5 Keep the dish in a warming drawer or very low oven or serve at once.

Facing page 96, dishes from *Pakistan and the Punjab*   Clockwise from top: Guchi Ka Pullao (page 131), Phulka bread (page 147), Tandoori Potato (page 124), Lobia Gogli (page 106), Chatt (page 159), Pali Dahi (page 111)

Opposite, dishes from *Nepal and North India*   Clockwise from top: Chyau (page 88), Roghni Naan bread (page 142), Hara Mattar Pati (page 67), Tamako Achar (page 163), Toovar Ke Malai (page 103)

Sayurmi Kari

Noodles with Mangetout, Green Beans and Coconut

Noodles are normally associated with Chinese cooking and they do not appear in traditional Indian recipes. But go to the countries between China and India and you will find fascinating spicy dishes majoring in noodles. This Indonesian recipe typifies that cultural and culinary confluence in a tasty combination. Non-vegans could use egg noodles instead of rice noodles.

SERVES: 4   V

6 oz (175 g) green beans, fresh or frozen
half a fresh coconut and its water or 2 oz (50 g) coconut milk powder
7 oz (200 g) rice noodles
4 tablespoons vegetable or coconut oil
2 teaspoons garlic purée
2 teaspoons ginger purée

8 oz (225 g) onion purée
6 oz (175 g) mangetout, stalks removed
6–10 fresh or dried curry leaves
2–6 dried red chillies, chopped
soy sauce to taste
salt to taste

1 Clean, string and slice the fresh beans or thaw the frozen beans, then boil them until soft.

2 Grind the coconut flesh and its water in an electric blender or food processor or by hand, or mix the coconut milk powder with enough water to make a paste.

3 Boil the noodles according to the instructions on the packet. Drain and set aside.

4 Heat half the oil in a *karahi* or wok. Stir-fry the garlic, ginger and onion purées for about 5 minutes.

5 During stage 4, heat the remaining oil in a separate pan and stir-fry the mangetout, curry leaves and red chillies for about 5 minutes. Add them to the stir-fry.

6 Add the fresh coconut purée or coconut milk paste, the soy sauce and sufficient water to prevent sticking. Add salt to taste.

7 Add the green beans and, when hot, add the noodles and mix well. Serve immediately they are heated through.

CHAPTER SIX

Legume Dishes

Legumes are the family of vegetables which include beans, lentils and peas. In certain cases the pods as well as the seeds (called pulses) are edible, and they are eaten fresh. More importantly these seeds can be dried, in which form they can be stored for months or years. The technology for this process has been practised for thousands of years, and it is simple. The pulses are picked, podded and spread out to dry in the hot sun for a few days. It is for this reason that pulses should be carefully picked over before using, as it is not uncommon to find small stones and pieces of grit amongst the seeds. The bigger producers now use convection ovens to dry the pulses, but even so you should still examine them first. Chickpeas are particularly prone to this problem.

To reconstitute pulses it is necessary to soak them. The larger and harder the pulse, the longer the soak. Chickpeas and red kidney beans, for example, need 12 hours or more. In certain cases the soaking and subsequent rinsing removes minor toxins. Red kidney beans must always be fast boiled for 10 minutes at the start of the cooking process to rid them of toxins.

The range of pulses is enormous. Not only are they remarkably high in nutritional value but they are filling and, with spices and other flavourings added, extremely tasty.

Maushawa

Red Kidney Beans with Black and Green Lentils

This is a very nutritious dish from Afghanistan. In this vegetarian version three legumes are united in a spicy sour sauce in which yoghurt plays its part. It makes an admirable main course dish and I love it served with plain rice.

SERVES: 4

3 oz (75g) red kidney beans
4 oz (110g) whole black urid dhal
4 oz (110g) whole green moong dhal
4 tablespoons vegetable oil
8 oz (225g) onion, finely chopped
1 red pepper
2–4 fresh green chillies (optional)
4–6 tomatoes

5 oz (125g) yoghurt
2–3 teaspoons garam masala
aromatic salt to taste

Spices
1 teaspoon cummin seeds
1 teaspoon ground coriander
1 teaspoon paprika

1 Soak the red kidney beans overnight, then rinse several times next day and drain. Soak the two dhals together, also overnight, then rinse and drain.

2 Boil the kidney beans in ample water for about 1 hour, or until soft. Drain.

3 At the same time, boil the two dhals in ample water in a separate pan for about 40 minutes. Drain.

4 During stages 2 and 3, heat the oil in a *karahi* or wok and stir-fry the onion for about 5 minutes. Add the **spices** and continue to stir-fry for a further 3 or 4 minutes.

5 Purée the red pepper, optional chillies and tomatoes in a blender and add them to the pan. Stir-fry for about 5 more minutes.

6 Add the beans and dhals, yoghurt and sufficient water to make the mixture neither sticky nor runny. Add the garam masala and salt to taste.

Sabzi Paneer Dhansak
—•—

Mixed Vegetables in a Lentil Purée

*D*hansak is a Parsee dish and probably their most celebrated. The lentil purée is augmented with tomatoes, aubergines and spinach, and traditionally cooked in that would be lamb. In this vegetarian version I have substituted a combination of mixed root vegetables and deep-fried paneer (Indian cheese). The latter can be omitted by vegans or to simplify the cooking, in which case add the equivalent weight of extra vegetables. Serve with Indian bread and/or brown rice.

SERVES: 4

6 oz (175 g) red (masoor) lentils
2 oz (50 g) turnip, scraped and diced
2 oz (50 g) parsnip, scraped and diced
2 oz (50 g) carrot, scraped and diced
4 tablespoons vegetable ghee or oil
2–4 cloves garlic, finely chopped
4 oz (110 g) onion, finely chopped
14 oz (400 g) can tomatoes and their juice
1 tablespoon finely chopped red pepper
1 tablespoon finely chopped green pepper
4 oz (110 g) aubergine, finely chopped
4 oz (110 g) fresh or frozen spinach leaves, chopped

2 tablespoons mild curry paste
2 tablespoons coconut milk powder
4 tablespoons finely chopped fresh coriander
2 tablespoons finely chopped fresh mint or 2 teaspoons dried mint
aromatic salt to taste
4 oz (110 g) pre-fried paneer cubes (page 36) and/or 2 oz (50 g) raw cashew nuts

Spices
1 teaspoon cummin seeds
1 teaspoon mustard seeds
4 inch (10 cm) piece cassia bark
6 green cardamoms

1 Pick through the lentils to remove any grit or impurities. Rinse them, then drain and soak for about 4 hours.

2 Drain and rinse the lentils.

3 Measure twice the drained lentils' volume of water into a 4 pint (2·25 litre) saucepan and bring to the boil.

4 Put in the lentils and simmer for about 30 minutes, stirring as the water is absorbed.

5 During stage 4, bring another 4 pints (2·25 litres) of water to the boil and cook the turnip, parsnip and carrot for about 20 minutes. Drain and add to the lentil pan.

6 Also during stage 4, heat the ghee or oil in a *karahi* or wok. Stir-fry the **spices** for 1 minute, then add the garlic, stir-frying for a further minute. Add the onion and stir-fry for a further 4–5 minutes.

7 Add the tomatoes and their juice, the red and green peppers, aubergine and spinach and simmer for about 10 minutes.

8 Add these to the lentils at the end of their 30 minutes' simmering time (stage 4).

9 Mix in the curry paste, coconut milk powder, fresh coriander, mint and salt to taste. Also add the pre-fried paneer and/or cashew nuts.

10 Cook for a further 10 minutes, ensuring it does not stick to the bottom of the pan. (Add a little water if it does.) Then serve hot with Indian bread and/or rice.

Toovar Ke Malai

Oily Dhal with Cream

I was invited to the London home of the Nawab (or Prince) Ahmed Husain and his wife the Begum for a wonderful meal. He is related to the former royal family of Hyderabad, and can trace his ancestry directly back to the Moghul emperors. He and his wife are great gourmets and cooks, a fact which would make his royal ancestors turn in their graves. Cooking was for the servants!

The Nawab's recipes are from the royal kitchens, and are themselves descended from the Moghuls. This fabulous creamy dhal recipe is one of them.

SERVES: 4

8 oz (225 g) toovar dhal
4 tablespoons vegetable ghee
2–4 cloves garlic, finely chopped
3 fl oz (85 ml) single cream
1 teaspoon saffron in kewra water
(page 20)
aromatic salt to taste
1 tablespoon chopped fresh coriander
leaves
sprinkling of onion tarka for garnish

Spices
1 teaspoon ground cummin
½ teaspoon turmeric
⅛ teaspoon asafoetida
chilli powder to taste

1 Pick through the lentils to remove any grit or impurities. Rinse them, then drain and soak for 1 hour. Drain and rinse them again.

2 Measure twice the drained lentils' volume of water into a 4 pint (2·25 litre) saucepan and bring to the boil. Put in the lentils and simmer for about 45 minutes or until very soft, stirring as the water is absorbed.

3 During stage 2, heat the ghee in a *karahi* or wok and stir-fry the garlic for 1 minute. Add the **spices** and stir-fry for a further minute. Remove from the heat and, when coolish, add the cream and saffron.

4 When the toovar dhal has reduced to a purée, add the creamy contents of the *karahi*. Add salt to taste and the fresh coriander and bring to a simmer. Serve hot, garnished with crispy *tarka* onions.

Papiroo

Sri Lankan Spicy Lentils with Cashews

Cashew nuts grow profusely in Sri Lanka and, along with the particular spices, the coconut flavouring makes this dish distinctive.

SERVES: 4   V

8 oz (225 g) polished moong dhal
4 tablespoons coconut or sunflower oil
4 oz (110 g) onions, finely chopped
6 oz (175 g) cashew nuts
1½ oz (40 g) coconut milk powder
2 tablespoons desiccated coconut
aromatic salt to taste
2 tablespoons finely chopped fresh
*   coriander leaves*

Spices
2 teaspoons mustard seeds
1 teaspoon turmeric
⅛ teaspoon asafoetida
6–10 curry leaves, fresh or dried
2–6 dried red chillies, chopped

1 Pick through the lentils to remove any grit or impurities, then soak them in ample water for about 4 hours. Drain, rinse several times and drain again.

2 Measure twice the drained lentils' volume of water into a 4 pint (2·25 litre) saucepan and bring to the boil.

3 Put in the lentils and simmer for about 30 minutes, stirring as the water is absorbed.

4 During stage 3, heat the oil in a *karahi* or wok and stir-fry the **spices** for 1 minute. Add the onions and stir-fry for about 5 minutes. Add the cashew nuts and stir-fry on a lowish heat for about 10 minutes or until the nuts become dark gold in colour.

5 Also during stage 3, mix the coconut milk powder with enough water to make a thinnish paste. Add it to the stir-fry with the desiccated coconut. When it begins to simmer, add the stir-fry to the lentil pan.

6 Stir in and cook until the lentils are a soft purée. Add salt to taste and serve garnished with the fresh coriander.

Missayeko Dal Haru

Nepalese Mixed Lentils

In Nepal these lentils are either eaten freshly picked, when they are lovely and soft, or in the more familiar dried form. I have never been able to obtain these legumes fresh outside the sub-continent, so we must use dried lentils. There is a difference, of course, but who is to say which is better? Here I use the standard dried lentils.

SERVES: 4   V

2 oz (50 g) whole black urid dhal
2 oz (50 g) whole red masoor dhal
2 oz (50 g) whole green moong dhal
2 oz (50 g) split yellow chana dhal
4 tablespoons vegetable ghee or oil
2–4 cloves garlic, finely chopped
1 inch (2·5 cm) cube fresh ginger,
  finely chopped
4 oz (110 g) onions, finely chopped
aromatic salt to taste

2 tablespoons finely chopped fresh
  coriander leaves

Spices
1 teaspoon ground cummin
1 teaspoon ground coriander
1 teaspoon garam masala
½ teaspoon turmeric
½–1 teaspoon chilli powder

1 Pick through the lentils to remove any grit or impurities, then mix them together and soak for at least 4 hours. Drain, rinse several times, then drain again.

2 Measure twice the drained lentils' volume of water into a 4 pint (2·25 litre) saucepan and bring to the boil.

3 Put in the lentils and simmer for about 30 minutes, stirring as the water is absorbed.

4 During stage 3, heat the oil in a *karahi* or wok. Stir-fry the garlic, ginger and onion for about 10 minutes. Add the **spices** and continue to stir-fry for about 5 more minutes. (Add a little water to prevent sticking.)

5 Add the stir-fry to the lentils. Mix well, adding salt to taste. Serve garnished with the fresh coriander leaves.

Lobia Gogli

Black-Eyed Beans with Turnips

The ivory-coloured lobia bean, with its little black eye, is attractive and makes a pleasant change. This spicy Pakistani recipe includes turnips and it makes a nourishing main course dish or accompaniment served with rice and/or Indian bread.

SERVES: 4

10 oz (300 g) black-eyed lobia beans
4 tablespoons vegetable ghee or oil
2–4 teaspoons garlic purée
2–4 teaspoons ginger purée
4 oz (110 g) onion, finely chopped
6 oz (175 g) turnip, cleaned and diced
*   into 1 inch (2·5 cm) cubes*
3 fl oz (85 ml) natural yoghurt

aromatic salt to taste
several sprigs fresh dill for garnish

Spices
2 teaspoons sesame seeds
2 teaspoons poppy seeds
1 teaspoon cummin seeds

1 Pick through the beans to remove any grit or impurities. Rinse, drain, then soak in ample water for about 4 hours. Discard any floating beans, drain, rinse several times and drain again.

2 Bring about 2 pints (1·2 litres) of water to the boil in a 4 pint (2·25 litre) saucepan. Put in the beans and boil for about 45 minutes. Check from time to time that all is well.

3 During stage 2, heat the oil in a *karahi* or wok. Stir-fry the **spices** for 1 minute, then add the garlic and fry for a further minute, the ginger and fry for another minute, and the onion and fry for about a further 5 minutes.

4 Also during stage 2, boil the diced turnips for about 15 minutes or until soft, then drain.

5 When the lobia are soft, drain them and combine them with the stir-fry and the turnips in the 4 pint (2·25 litre) pan and stir-fry until hot. Add the yoghurt and salt to taste. Add water to obtain the texture you require.

6 Serve garnished with the fresh dill sprigs.

Molaghashyam

Lentils, Vegetables and Coconut Curry

This typically South Indian dish consists of a creamy spicy lentil curry with shallots, aubergine and coconut milk, which you can make very mild or as hot as you wish. It is equally delicious served on its own with rice and chutneys, or as an accompaniment. It freezes very well, losing none of its original flavour or texture when reheated.

SERVES: 4 as an accompaniment   V

6 oz (175 g) toovar or toor dhal
2 oz (50 g) chickpeas (kabli chana)
3 tablespoons vegetable or mustard oil
2 garlic cloves, chopped
2 inch (5 cm) piece fresh ginger, chopped
1 medium-sized onion, peeled and chopped
6 shallots or spring onions
2 tablespoons vinegar (any kind)
6 curry leaves, fresh or dried
2–4 green chillies
1 small aubergine, chopped

6–8 fl oz (175–250 g) coconut milk
  or 2 tablespoons coconut milk powder mixed with water
2 tablespoons chopped fresh coriander leaves

Spices (ground)
2 teaspoons coriander
1 teaspoon cummin
$\frac{1}{2}$ teaspoon turmeric
$\frac{1}{2}$ teaspoon fenugreek seeds
$\frac{1}{4}$ teaspoon asafoetida
1 teaspoon chilli powder (optional)

1 Pick through the toovar dhal to remove any grit or impurities, then rinse well. Leave to soak in ample water overnight. Do the same with the chickpeas, keeping them separate.

2 Prior to cooking drain and rinse both, then measure out approximately twice their volumes of water and bring to the boil in separate saucepans. When boiling, add the pulses and cook until each is tender (about 45 minutes). The toovar will probably get there first. Add more water if needed.

3 Meanwhile, heat the oil, then fry in this order for 2–3 minutes each: the garlic, ginger and onion, then the shallots or spring onions, stirring frequently.

4 Mix the **spices** with the vinegar to form a loose paste, then add to the frying pan and cook for 5 minutes.

5 Add the curry leaves, chillies and aubergine and fry a few minutes more, then combine all this in the toovar pan.

6 Add the drained chickpeas when they are ready. Add the coconut milk and salt to taste.

7 Garnish with a sprinkling of fresh coriander.

Kootoo Kari

Yam, Green Banana, Gourds and Chana Curry

In the Tamil language, *kootoo* means 'combination'. The dish is called *pitlai* in other southern Indian languages. The combination should contain two or three vegetables plus, often, a lentil. The ingredients in this version are typical, as are beans, aubergines and pepper. Gourds include any type of squash or marrow of all shapes and sizes.

SERVES: 4   V

2 oz (50 g) chana dhal
12–16 oz (350–450 g) spaghetti
   squash
8–12 oz (225–350 g) red sweet
   potatoes (American yams), peeled
6 tablespoons mustard oil
1 tablespoon mustard seeds
2–4 teaspoons garlic purée
6 tablespoons onion purée
2–4 fresh green chillies, chopped
½ green capsicum pepper, chopped

1–2 green bananas, chopped into discs
2 tablespoons chopped fresh coriander
   leaves
salt to taste

Spices
3 tablespoons coconut milk powder
2 tablespoons gram flour (besan)
½ teaspoon ground black pepper
½ teaspoon asafoetida

1 Pick through the chana dhal for grit and impurities, then soak in water for at least 6 hours (up to 18 hours). Rinse and drain.

2 Make a paste of the **spices** by adding water and leave it to stand for a while.

3 Boil the spaghetti squash in its skin in ample water for 20 minutes. Remove it and set aside until stage 6.

4 At the same time, separately boil the whole sweet potatoes for the same length of time. Drain and set aside.

5 Heat the oil in a *karahi* or wok. Fry the mustard seeds and the chana dhal for 3–4 minutes. Drain and set aside.

6 Reheat the oil and stir-fry the spice paste for 5 minutes, adding a little water as it thickens until it is creamy. Add the garlic and onion purées and stir-fry for about 5 more minutes. Add the chillies, green pepper, green banana and fresh coriander and, while heating, cut open the spaghetti squash and scoop the flesh into the *karahi*. Cut the sweet potatoes into 1 inch (2·5 cm) cubes and put them into the *karahi*. Stir-fry. Add enough water to create a thickish gravy. Add salt to taste and, when it is bubbling, serve garnished with the mustard seeds and chana.

CHAPTER SEVEN

Non-Vegan Dishes

Each of the following recipes contains one or more non-vegan ingredient, such as milk, cream, yoghurt, eggs, or honey. The use of these products is very widespread in the countries of the sub-continent. Significantly, the use of dairy products diminishes as one travels towards China. In Burma it is rare, whilst in Thailand and amongst certain groups of the populations of Malaysia and Indonesia it is non-existent. The reason for this is that the peoples of Chinese origin are unable to digest milk-based products.

The Thais adore eggs, however, and I have included a delightful spicy Thai omelette. The remaining recipes are mostly traditional Indian. As with the recipes in Chapter 5, feel free to change the principal ingredients to those of your choice as the mood takes you, to extend the range of possibilities available.

Sag or Palak Pachadi

Spinach in Yoghurt

This is a South Indian dish. It is a simple combination of spinach (*sag* or *palak*) and yoghurt, called in the south *pachadi* or *raita*. It can be served hot or cold.

SERVES: 4

1½ *lb (675 g) spinach leaves*
4 tablespoons mustard oil
2 teaspoons mustard seeds
2–4 cloves garlic, finely sliced
1 inch (2·5 cm) cube fresh ginger,
* finely sliced*

1–4 fresh green chillies, finely
* shredded (optional)*
1–2 tablespoons fresh coriander
* leaves*
5 fl oz (150 ml) natural yoghurt
aromatic salt to taste

1 Wash the spinach leaves very carefully, ensuring that all grit and soil is removed, then cut away the hard stalks, leaving the soft edible stalks. Coarsely chop the spinach.

2 Immerse it in ample boiling water and simmer for 10–15 minutes. Drain.

3 During stage 2, heat the oil in a *karahi* or wok. Stir-fry the mustard seeds for about 30 seconds; add the garlic, ginger and optional chillies and continue to stir-fry for about 3 more minutes.

4 Add the fresh coriander, stir and take off the heat until the spinach is drained.

5 Then return to the heat and add the spinach. Stir until it is sizzling, then add the yoghurt and salt to taste. Serve when hot, or allow to cool.

Pali Dahi

Green Beans in Yoghurt

In this Punjabi recipe, the fresh beans normally used are the long thin pods which contain black-eyed lobia beans. They grow up to 15 inches (38 cm) long and are available from time to time in the West, known as *asparagus beans*. They are also called *papyaru* in southern India. Fine substitutes are any snap beans, such as French or Kenyan beans, moguettes or cowpeas.

SERVES: 4

1 lb (450 g) French Kenyan or other
  snap beans
4 tablespoons vegetable ghee or oil
2–4 cloves garlic, finely chopped
1 inch (2·5 cm) cube fresh ginger,
  finely chopped
4 oz (110 g) onion, finely chopped
5 fl oz (150 ml) thick (Greek)
  natural yoghurt
aromatic salt to taste
2 teaspoons cummin seeds, roasted

1 teaspoon garam masala
1 tablespoon chopped fresh coriander
  leaves

Spices
1 teaspoon ground coriander
1 teaspoon ground cummin
½ teaspoon turmeric
¼ teaspoon ground fenugreek seeds
0–2 teaspoons chilli powder
  (optional)

1 Wash the beans and top and tail them. Snap beans should not have inedible strings, but check and remove if necessary. Cut them into about 2 inch (5 cm) pieces.

2 Immerse them in ample boiling water and simmer for about 10 minutes. Drain.

3 During stage 2, heat the oil in a *karahi* or wok. Stir-fry the **spices** for 1 minute, then add the garlic, ginger and onion and stir-fry for about 5 minutes.

4 Add the drained beans to the *karahi* with the yoghurt and salt to taste. Bring to a simmer and serve hot, garnishing with the roasted cummin seeds, garam masala and fresh coriander.

Mooli Maiwalla

White Radish with Coconut and Cream

The long white radish, resembling an elephant's tusk, was almost unknown in Britain a few years ago. Now it is readily available at greengrocers. And very versatile it is too, either raw or cooked as in this dish whose recipe I obtained in Madras.

SERVES: 4

1 lb (450g) mooli (white radish)
4 tablespoons mustard or coconut oil
2–4 teaspoons garlic purée
4 oz (110g) onion purée
2 oz (50g) coconut milk powder
3 fl oz (85 ml) single cream
2 or 3 fresh green chillies, chopped
  (optional)
3–4 tablespoons chopped fresh
  coriander leaves
some milk (possibly)
aromatic salt to taste

2–3 tablespoons fresh coconut flesh;
  grated or shredded,
  or 3–4 tablespoons desiccated
  coconut
2 teaspoons mustard seeds

Spices
1 teaspoon white cummin seeds
1 teaspoon mustard seeds
½ teaspoon fennel seeds
¼ teaspoon black cummin seeds

1 Scrape the mooli(s), top and tail and dice into cubes averaging ¾ inch (2 cm) in size.

2 Heat the oil in a *karahi* or wok and stir-fry the **spices** for 1 minute. Add the garlic and onion purées and stir-fry for about 5 minutes.

3 During stage 2, make a thinnish paste of coconut milk powder by adding water, then add in the cream. Add this to the stir-fry at the end of stage 2 and bring to a low simmer.

4 Add the mooli, the optional chillies and most of the fresh coriander and stir-fry for 5–8 minutes, ensuring the creamy sauce does not stick to the pan. If it does, add a little milk. Add salt to taste.

5 During stage 5, mix the fresh coconut or desiccated coconut with the mustard seeds and spread out on foil on the grill pan placed at the midway position. Roast under medium heat for a couple of minutes, until it is pale buff coloured.

6 Serve hot. The mooli should be nice and crispy, not mushy. Garnish with the roasted coconut and mustard seeds and the remaining fresh coriander leaves.

Bonjon-e-Burance

Aubergine in Yoghurt (Afghan)

Yoghurt is very popular in Afghanistan and this tasty dish combines it with aubergines. The uniqueness of the dish lies in the method of cooking the aubergines – they must be stir-fried. Boiling will, in this case, make them too mushy.

SERVES: 4

1 lb (450 g) shiny purple aubergines
juice of 1 lemon
2 teaspoons salt
4 tablespoons vegetable oil
8 oz (225 g) onion, finely chopped
5 fl oz (150 ml) natural yoghurt
some milk (possibly)
aromatic salt to taste

1 teaspoon chilli powder (optional)
1 teaspoon garam masala

Spices
1 teaspoon ground coriander
1 teaspoon ground cummin
½ teaspoon ground cassia or cinnamon

1 Cut the top husks off the aubergines and discard. Wash the aubergines and dice into cubes about ¾ inch (2 cm) in size. Place them in cold water into which the lemon juice has been squeezed and the salt dissolved. This prevents the aubergines from going brown and removes their bitter taste. Leave for an hour or so, then drain.

2 Heat the oil in a *karahi* or wok. Stir-fry the **spices** for 1 minute, then the onion for about 5 minutes.

3 Add about ⅓ of the drained aubergine cubes and stir-fry for 2–3 minutes. Drain the contents of the *karahi* and put aside for the moment.

4 Use the strained oil, plus a top-up as necessary, and repeat stage 3 twice more until all the aubergine cubes have been fried.

5 Now place them all back into the *karahi* and stir until they are all simmering.

6 Reduce the heat and add the yoghurt, stirring briskly (too much heat may cause it to curdle).

7 Simmer for about 15–20 minutes, then check the texture of the aubergine. It may well be cooked sufficiently to your liking, or you may wish to go on a little longer. If it wants to stick to the pan, add a little milk. Add salt to taste.

8 Serve hot, garnished with the optional chilli powder and garam masala.

Moghul Sabzi Korma

Exotic Vegetables Aromatically Spiced in Cream

The korma is one of the supreme dishes from the era of the Moghul emperors. It is aromatic, mild in heat level, creamy and is traditionally cooked with meat. Here I have used the traditional spice base with exotic vegetables.

SERVES: 4

1–1¼ lb (450–550 g) combination of vegetables of your choice, weighed after preparation (see stage 1 below)
4 tablespoons ghee or vegetable oil
2 teaspoons ginger purée
4 oz (110 g) onion purée
5 fl oz (150 ml) single cream
2 fl oz (50 ml) natural yoghurt
2–3 teaspoons white sugar (optional)
3–4 tablespoons finely chopped fresh coriander leaves
2–3 tablespoons finely chopped fresh parsley

some milk (possibly)
aromatic salt to taste
some onion tarka for garnish

Spices
seeds from four whole green cardamoms
4 or 5 whole cloves
1 inch (2·5 cm) piece cassia bark
1 teaspoon white cummin seeds
½ teaspoon fennel seeds
1 teaspoon turmeric
1 teaspoon ground coriander
1 teaspoon ground cassia or coriander

1 Choose any combination of exotic or other vegetables. It is best to include, say, four or five different vegetables of contrasting colours and textures – for example, red sweet potato (American yam), lilva beans, sarson (mustard) leaves, Jerusalem artichoke, carrot and peas.

2 Dice the vegetables that need it into smallish cubes.

3 Cook each separately to three-quarters tenderness, then drain and combine.

4 Heat the oil in a *karahi* or wok. Stir-fry the **spices** for 1 minute, then add the ginger and onion purées. Continue to stir-fry for 3–4 minutes.

5 Add the drained vegetables and stir-fry until well mixed but not too hot.

6 Then add the cream and yoghurt, optional sugar, most of the fresh coriander and the parsley.

7 Stir-fry until all is heated through and properly cooked. Add a little milk if it starts to thicken too much. Add salt to taste.

8 Serve hot, garnished with *tarka* onions and the remaining fresh coriander.

Makai Bhutta

Spicy Sweetcorn in Cream

I remember when I was a small boy my grandfather often wished he could have *bhutta* (pronounced *boota*). I had no idea what he was talking about. Then one day my mother grew some in the garden. It was sweetcorn and my grandpa was ecstatic, for this was his *boota* and he hadn't had any since he left India at least 20 years before. Now, of course, sweetcorn is readily available in the late summer. At that time it was fed to the pigs.

This northern Indian dish makes the most of the sweetcorn. Fresh is nicest, but canned or frozen is acceptable.

SERVES: 4

4 large cobs sweetcorn
4 tablespoons butter or ghee
8 oz (225 g) onion, finely chopped
5 fl oz (150 ml) single cream
2 fl oz (50 ml) natural yoghurt
2 teaspoons white sugar (optional)
2–4 green chillies, chopped
2 tablespoons whole fresh coriander
  leaves

salt to taste
freshly milled black pepper to taste

Spices
2 teaspoons sesame seeds
1 teaspoon white poppy seeds
$\frac{1}{2}$ teaspoon fennel seeds
$\frac{1}{4}$ teaspoon wild onion seeds
$\frac{1}{8}$ teaspoon asafoetida

1 Pick all the leaves and hairs off the sweetcorn cobs and rinse them.

2 Place them in an ample amount of boiling water and simmer for 15–20 minutes. Drain.

3 When cool enough to handle, hold the first cob base down on a chopping board and carefully cut down the cob so that as much as possible of each grain of corn comes away. Separate any grains that stick together.

4 Repeat stage 3 with the remaining cobs.

5 During stage 2, heat the butter or ghee and stir-fry the **spices** for about 30 seconds. Add the onion and continue to stir-fry for 3–4 minutes.

6 Remove from the heat and, when coolish, add the cream, yoghurt, optional sugar, optional fresh chillies and fresh coriander. Stir in well.

7 Bring back to a simmer and, when simmering, add the sweetcorn grains. Stir well and, when heated through, add salt to taste.

8 Serve hot, garnished with freshly milled black pepper.

Malai Looki Kofta

Marrow and Melon Balls in Cream

Koftas are small balls. This delicious kofta from a central Indian household uses a remarkable combination of marrow and melon. The small 'dumplings' can be steamed or deep-fried. I prefer the latter for flavour but, either way, the koftas must be light and very freshly cooked. They are immersed in a spicy creamy curry gravy and served with rice and chutneys to make a substantial main course dish.

SERVES: 4

The Batter
4 oz (110 g) gram flour
2 oz (50 g) coconut milk powder
2 oz (50 g) plain white flour
3 teaspoons mild curry powder
½ teaspoon mango powder
juice of 1 lemon
1 teaspoon salt
1 teaspoon white sugar

The Filling
12 oz (350 g) marrow
6 oz (175 g) melon (about ½ melon)
vegetable oil for deep-frying

The Gravy
4 tablespoons ghee or vegetable oil
2 teaspoons garlic purée
2 teaspoons ginger purée
4 oz (110 g) onion purée
1–2 tablespoons curry paste
2 teaspoons tomato paste
5 fl oz (150 ml) single cream
2 fl oz (50 ml) natural yoghurt
2 tablespoons finely chopped fresh coriander
milk if needed
aromatic salt to taste

1 Make the batter first by mixing the dry ingredients with the lemon juice and enough water to make a stiff texture which eventually drops off the spoon. Leave the batter to stand for up to 30 minutes to allow it to absorb the moisture effectively.

2 During that time, turn your attention to the marrow and melon.

3 Cut the marrow in half, discard the pips etc., then scoop out the flesh and chop it finely. Place it into a strainer so that the excess liquid drains off. Keep the liquid for later.

4 Repeat stage 3 with the melon.

5 Mix the marrow and melon into the batter at the end of its 30-minute rest.

6 Mix well. If the mixture is now sliding quickly off the spoon, thicken it with some extra flour until it only just drops off.

7 Heat the deep-fryer to 340°F/170°C.

8 Sprinkle some plain flour on a work surface. Scoop out a dollop of mixture about 1 inch (2·5 cm) in diameter and lightly roll it into a ball.

9 Repeat until all the mixture is used. You should have about 24 balls, depending on their size.

10 Carefully place 12 balls into the fryer one at a time. They will sink at first, then bob up to the surface. Fry them for about 10 minutes, turning them at least once so that they cook evenly.

11 Remove and place on kitchen paper.

12 Repeat stages 10 and 11 with the remaining balls.

13 During stages 10–12, make the gravy. Heat the oil in a *karahi* or wok and stir-fry the garlic, ginger and onion purées for about 10 minutes.

14 Add the curry and tomato pastes and stir-fry well. Take off the heat and allow to cool down a little. Then add the cream, yoghurt and liquid from stage 3.

15 When all the balls are fried, return the *karahi* to the heat and bring the gravy to a gentle simmer.

16 Add the balls to the gravy with the fresh coriander. Stir carefully while the balls are heating through (about 8 to 10 minutes). Add a little milk if the sauce thickens too much. Add salt to taste and serve at once.

Paneer Ke Shakerland

Fried Cheese and Sweet Potato or Yam Curry

This is a dish of interesting tastes and textures. Both the paneer and the sweet potato or yam are deep-fried. Both become gorgeously crunchy, and you have the added bonus of a sweet taste from the potato or yam. The savoury gravy coordinates the whole into a fine main course dish.

SERVES: 4

*1 quantity deep-fried paneer (see
    stage 1)
8–10 oz (225–300 g) white sweet
    potatoes or yams
4 tablespoons ghee or vegetable oil
2–4 tablespoons garlic purée
4 oz (110 g) onion purée
¼ pint (150 ml) milk
2 tablespoons tomato purée
vegetable oil for deep-frying
aromatic salt to taste*

*Spices
2 tablespoons ground coriander
1 teaspoon ground cummin
1 teaspoon turmeric
1 teaspoon garam masala
1 teaspoon paprika
2 teaspoons dried fenugreek leaves*

1 Prepare the paneer as described on page 36. Remember this stage will require initial preparations some 6 hours ahead. Do the actual frying of the paneer at stage 5 below to achieve maximum crispness.

2 Scrub the sweet potatoes or yams, removing unwanted matter, and scrape or peel them. Dice into cubes the same size as the paneer.

3 Heat the oil in a *karahi* or wok and stir-fry the garlic and onion purées for about 5 minutes. Add the **spices** and continue for another 5 minutes.

4 Bit by bit as the mixture thickens, add the milk. It will give a good creamy consistency if done slowly. Then add the tomato purée.

5 During stage 3, heat the deep-fryer to 375°F/190°C and, when hot, immerse the paneer and fry for about 5 minutes, until evenly golden. Drain.

6 Follow with the potato or yam, cooked for the same length of time. Drain.

7 Add the deep-fried paneer and potato or yam to the *karahi*. Adjust the thickness of the sauce by adding a little water as needed. Add salt to taste and serve when hot.

Methi Chaaman

Fenugreek, Spinach and Indian Cheese

In this fine Kashmiri recipe the Indian cheese, called *chaaman* in Kashmir, is used in crumbly form and not cubed and fried. I had this dish served to me on a beautiful sandalwood houseboat on the Dal Lake in Srinagar, Kashmir's capital. The boat was exquisitely carved and the wood itself had a divine fragrance. Couple that with the tempting aromas of this dish and you know that the emperor Shah Jahan was right when he said, 'If there is a heaven on earth, this is it.'

SERVES: 4

$1\frac{1}{2}$ lb (675 g) spinach leaves
2–4 cloves of garlic
4 tablespoons natural yoghurt
1 tablespoon fresh coriander leaves
2–4 fresh green chillies (optional)
3 tablespoons ghee or vegetable oil
8 oz (225 g) crumbled Indian cheese
aromatic salt to taste
akhni stock or water as required

Spices
2–4 tablespoons dried fenugreek
leaves
1 tablespoon coriander seeds
1 teaspoon cummin seeds
2–4 whole black/brown cardamoms
4–6 whole cloves

1 Rinse the spinach until you are certain any soil or grit is removed. Discard any coarse stems. Drain and coarsely chop.

2 Boil it in ample water for about 15 minutes. Drain.

3 During stage 2, roast and finely grind the **spices** (page 24).

4 Put the **spices**, a couple of tablespoons of cooked spinach, the garlic, yoghurt, fresh coriander and optional chillies into a blender or food processor and blend to a smooth paste.

5 Heat the ghee or oil in a *karahi* or wok and carefully (to avoid spluttering) put the paste into the oil. Stir-fry for 6–8 minutes, adding enough water to prevent sticking.

6 Add the remainder of the spinach and stir-fry until it is well mixed and heated through.

7 Add the crumbled Indian cheese and mix in well. Add salt to taste.

8 The dish will be fairly dry by now, so add akhni stock or water if you want a runnier texture. Serve when hot.

Kalan

Mango and Gourds in Beaten Curd

This southern Indian curry is an absolute delight. The curds (yoghurt) give it a creamy sour sauce, coloured by the spices. This is enhanced by coconut paste.

When I first had this dish, tiny mangoes resembling small plums were used. They are nigh on impossible to get in the West, so I have used firm full-sized mangoes, the flesh of which is scooped out with a melon baller. The original recipe used ash gourds, which are occasionally available in specialist markets, but any pumpkin, gourd or marrow can be substituted. This dish is also sometimes called *Pachadi*.

SERVES: 4

4–6 firm mangoes
1–1½ lb (450–675 g) marrow
4 tablespoons mustard oil
1 tablespoon mustard seeds
1 inch (2·5 cm) cube fresh ginger,
    finely sliced

0–4 fresh green chillies, chopped
    (optional)
5 fl oz (150 ml) natural yoghurt
salt to taste

1 Halve the mangoes, stone them and scoop out small balls of flesh with a melon baller. Use any pulp or odd shapes as well. Discard the skins.

2 Boil or bake the marrow for about 20 minutes. Cool it enough to enable you to cut it open and cut the flesh into cubes. Discard the seeds, pith and skin.

3 During stage 2, heat the oil in a *karahi* or wok. Stir-fry the mustard seeds for 1 minute; add the ginger and the optional chillies and continue stir-frying for a minute more.

4 Beat the yoghurt briskly with a fork or whisk. Add it to the *karahi*, stirring rapidly to prevent it from curdling. Straight away add the marrow and, when it is simmering, add the mango. Add a little water if needed and salt to taste. Serve when hot.

Andai Bandai

Quail or Other Hard-Boiled Egg Curry

Quail eggs are so pretty, and they look very good indeed in this Moghul recipe. But if you cannot obtain them, use chicken or duck eggs, allowing 2 per person as a main course dish. I have incorporated cherry tomatoes into this recipe. They match the quails eggs in size and contrast with them perfectly in colour.

SERVES: 4

12–16 quail eggs
2 tablespoons ghee or vegetable oil
1 teaspoon garlic purée
1 teaspoon ginger purée
4 oz (110 g) onion purée
1 cupful akhni stock or water
1–2 fresh green chillies (optional)
1 tablespoon fresh coriander leaves
8–16 cherry tomatoes
aromatic salt to taste

Spices 1
1 teaspoon cummin seeds
1 teaspoon mustard seeds
½ teaspoon aniseed

Spices 2
2 teaspoons mild curry powder
1 teaspoon garam masala
1 teaspoon dried mint
1 teaspoon dried fenugreek leaves
1 teaspoon chilli powder (optional)

1 Hard-boil the quail eggs – they only take about 4 minutes. Shell and set aside.

2 Heat the oil in a *karahi* or wok. Stir-fry **spices 1** for 1 minute, then add the garlic and fry for a further minute, the ginger and fry for another minute and the onion and fry for about 5 minutes. Add **spices 2** and stir-fry for 3–4 more minutes.

3 Add the akhni stock or water and bring to a simmer, stirring.

4 Add the optional chillies, fresh coriander leaves, hard-boiled eggs and the tomatoes.

5 When the curry simmers again, add salt to taste.

6 Serve at once.

Kai Yad Sai

Thai Savoury Spicy Omelette

This simple omelette is from Thailand. It is quick to make and is very tasty. Serve as part of a main meal, or as a snack with a salad accompaniment. In this form you may enjoy making a typical Thai vegetable carving to highlight the dish, and a rather original idea follows this recipe.

SERVES: 4

2 or 3 sticks celery
3–4 inch (7·5–10 cm) piece mooli
  (white radish)
⅓ red pepper
⅓–½ green pepper
2 or 3 tomatoes
1–4 fresh green chillies (optional)
2 tablespoons sunflower oil
2–4 teaspoons garlic purée
1–2 teaspoons ginger purée

2 oz (50 g) onion, finely chopped
splash of soy sauce
salt to taste
8 free-range eggs
2 tablespoons coconut milk powder
ground black pepper
1–2 tablespoons finely chopped fresh
  coriander leaves
butter as needed

1 Prepare and very finely chop the celery, mooli, red and green peppers, tomatoes and optional chillies.

2 Heat the oil in a *karahi* or wok. Stir-fry the garlic, ginger and onion for 3–4 minutes.

3 Add the finely chopped vegetables and, when they start to sizzle, splash in the soy sauce. Stir-fry until the mixture is soft and dryish (about 5 minutes). Add salt to taste.

4 During stages 2 and 3, whisk the eggs in a bowl. Add the coconut powder, black pepper and fresh coriander and mix in well.

5 Next heat a dab of butter in a flat frying pan. When it is melted, pour off the excess into the *karahi*.

6 Give the egg mixture a final brisk whisk, then pour one quarter of it into the frying pan. Deftly roll the egg mixture around the pan with a quick wrist action.

7 As soon as the eggs begin to set firmly, spoon a generous layer of the stir-fry mixture on top of the omelette.

8 Cook for about a minute longer, then slide the omelette out of the pan, roll it up and keep it warm.

9 Repeat stages 5 to 8 three more times to make a total of four omelettes. Freeze any spare filling.

Swan Garnish

Thai food is often served with carvings made from vegetables. These range from flowers to fish and animals, and are extraordinarily deft and artistic.

Here is a gorgeous carving made from a white radish, with a beak made from a piece of carrot. It is a swan. I saw it at a rather good restaurant called *Yum Yums* in Wandsworth.

MAKES: one swan

1 piece mooli (white radish) about 3–
4 inches (7·5–10 cm) by 2–2½
inches (5–6·5 cm) in diameter

1 tiny piece carrot
3 cocktail sticks

1 Peel the mooli as smoothly as possible.

2 Cut off 2 strips of mooli and carve them into wing shapes.

3 With a sharp paring knife, carve the head, neck and body in one piece, flattening the base so that it won't roll over.

4 Cut 2 slots in the back to fit the wings.

5 Cut the carrot into a beak shape.

6 Fit cocktail sticks into the beak and wing roots.

7 Assemble the swan and keep in cold water until needed.

8 Present the swan on a sea of chopped parsley and salad pieces.

Tandoori Potato

Tandoori dishes originated in the area that is now called Pakistan. It is a Moslem heartland, and as the people there are great meat eaters there are no vegetarian tandoori dishes. That is a great omission, in my opinion, and in this recipe I have attempted to redress the balance by using baked potatoes. The result, I hope you will agree, is most acceptable. It is important to achieve a good long marination to enable the tandoori flavours to permeate the potato as much as possible. Then, hey presto, you have a wonderful tasty snack or accompaniment.

SERVES: 4

4 large baking potatoes
juice of 1 lemon

The Marinade
5 fl oz (150 g) natural yoghurt
3 tablespoons mustard oil
1 teaspoon garlic purée
1 teaspoon ginger purée
1 tablespoon finely chopped fresh mint
   or 1 teaspoon bottled mint

3 tablespoons finely chopped fresh
   coriander leaves
1 teaspoon roasted cummin seed,
   ground
1 teaspoon garam masala
1 tablespoon mild curry paste
2 tablespoons tandoori dry mix
   masala
1 teaspoon salt

1 Mix the marinade ingredients together thoroughly.

2 Scrub and peel the potatoes, then poke them deeply with a small thin-bladed knife to assist the marinade to penetrate.

3 Rub each potato with lemon juice. This adds flavour and helps the marinade to adhere.

4 Coat each potato with $\frac{1}{4}$ of the marinade, then wrap each potato carefully in foil.

5 Place the potatoes on an oven tray and bake for 1–1$\frac{1}{4}$ hours in an oven pre-heated to 325°F/160°C/Gas 3.

6 Unwrap the potatoes and, keeping them on their foil, put them under the grill at medium heat to finish them off. Just cook them until they blacken a little bit, turning once.

7 Serve hot, on a bed of salad, with chutneys and Indian breads.

CHAPTER EIGHT

Rice Dishes

Rice is the most important staple in Asia. Indeed it is the only staple in southern India, Burma, Thailand, Malaysia and Indonesia. It would be hard to contemplate eating curry without rice.

There are many species of rice, but the best and most fragrant of them all is basmati rice. This is a thin long-grained rice which cooks relatively quickly and has a particularly delicious aroma. It also achieves the fluffiest, most separate grains if cooked properly. I use it in all the recipes which follow. Patna rice is another good long-grained rice, but it does not have quite the same fragrance or cooking properties as basmati.

Short-grained, round and glutinous rice varieties will not produce satisfactory results and 'quick cook' rice should, in my view, be avoided altogether. In this case the grains of rice are processed in the factory. The outer skin is milled off, enabling the rice to be cooked more quickly. The problem is that most of the goodness of the rice lies in the outer skin.

Rice is perfectly acceptable cooked by itself, but it is even nicer when combined with other ingredients. The recipes which follow include a very wide range of traditional flavourings which are rarely, if ever, encountered in the West.

I make no apology for reprinting from *The Curry Club Favourite Restaurant Curries* the two basic methods of cooking rice. If you are not experienced in rice cooking, it is well worth spending time over these two basic recipes. Once mastered, you will always produce perfect, fluffy, dry, tasty rice.

Plain Rice by Boiling

This is the quickest way to cook rice, and it can be ready to serve in just 15 minutes from the water boiling. Two factors are crucial for this method to work perfectly. Firstly, the rice must be basmati rice. Patna or long-grained, quick-cook or other rices, will require different timings and will have neither the texture nor the fragrance of basmati. Secondly, it is one of the few recipes in this book which requires *precision timing*. It is essential that for its few minutes on the boil you concentrate on it or else it may overcook and become stodgy.

A 3 oz (75 g) portion of dry rice provides an ample helping per person; 2 oz (50 g) will be a smaller but adequate portion.

SERVES: 4   V

8–12 oz (225–350 g) basmati rice
2–3 pints (1·2–1·8 litres) water

1 Pick through the rice to remove grit and impurities.

2 Boil the water. It is not necessary to salt it.

3 While it is heating up, rinse the rice briskly with fresh cold water until most of the starch is washed out. Run hot tap water through the rice at the final rinse. This minimises the temperature reduction of the boiling water when you put the rice into it.

4 When the water is boiling properly, put the rice into the pan. Start timing. Put the lid on the pan until the water comes back to the boil, then remove the lid. It takes 8–10 minutes from the start. Stir frequently.

5 After about 6 minutes, taste a few grains. As soon as the centre is no longer brittle but still has a good *al dente* bite to it, drain off the water. The rice should seem slightly *under*cooked.

6 Shake off all excess water, then place the strainer on to a dry tea towel which will help remove the last of the water.

7 After a minute place the rice in a warmed serving dish. You can serve it now or, preferably, put it into a very low oven or warming drawer for at least ½ hour. As it dries, the grains will separate and become fluffy. It can be held in the warmer for several hours if needed.

Plain Rice by Absorption

Cooking rice in a pre-measured ratio of water which is all absorbed into the rice is undoubtedly the best way to do it. Providing that you use basmati rice, the finished grains are longer, thinner and much more fragrant and flavourful than they are after boiling.

The method is easy, but many cookbooks make it sound far too complicated. Instructions invariably state that you must use a tightly lidded pot and precise water quantity and heat levels, and never lift the lid during the boiling process, etc., etc. However, I lift the lid, I might stir the rice, and I've even cooked rice by absorption without a lid. Also, if I've erred on the side of too little water, I've added a bit during 'the boil'. (Too much water is an unresolvable problem, however.) It's all naughty, rule-breaking stuff, but it still seems to work.

Another factor, always omitted in other people's books, is the time factor. They all say or imply that rice must be served as soon as 'the boil' is completed. This causes stress to the cook who believes that there is no margin of error in time and method. In reality, the longer you give the rice to dry, the fluffier and more fragrant it will be. So it can be cooked well in advance of being required for serving. For after the initial 'boil' and 10-minute simmer the rice is quite sticky, and it needs to 'relax'. After 30 minutes it can be served and is fluffy, but it can be kept in a warm place for much longer – improving the fluffiness all the time.

Cooking rice does need practice. You may need one or two goes at it. Here are some tips for the newcomer.

1 Choose a pan, preferably with a lid, that can be used both on the stove and in the oven. Until you have had lots of practice, always use the same pan so that you become familiar with it.

2 Keep a good eye on the clock. The timing of 'the boil' is important or you'll burn the bottom of the rice.

3 Use basmati rice.

4 If you intend to let the rice cool down for serving later or the next day, or to freeze it, do not put it in the warmer. It is better slightly undercooked for these purposes.

Note: 10 oz (300 g) is 2 teacups dry rice, and 20 fl oz (1 pint/570 ml) is about $1\frac{1}{3}$ volume of water to 1 of rice. This 10:20 (2 teacups:1 pint) combination is easy to remember, but do step up or step down the quantities as required in proportion. For small appetites, for instance, use 8 oz (225 g) rice:16 fl oz (450 ml) water. For large appetites use 12 oz (350 g) rice: 24 fl oz (685 ml) water.

SERVES: 4   [V]

10 oz (300 g) basmati rice
20 fl oz (1 pint/570 ml) water

1 Soak the rice in water to cover for about ½ hour.

2 Rinse it until the rinse water runs more or less clear, then drain.

3 Bring the measured water to the boil in a saucepan (as heavy as possible, and with a lid) or casserole dish with a capacity at least twice the volume of the drained rice.

4 As soon as it is boiling add the rice and stir in well.

5 As soon as it starts bubbling put the lid on the pan and reduce the heat to under half. Leave well alone for 8 minutes.

6 Inspect. Has the liquid on top been absorbed? If not, replace the lid and leave for 2 more minutes. If and when it has, stir the rice well, ensuring that it is not sticking to the bottom. Now taste. It should not be brittle in the middle. If it is, add a little more water and return to the heat.

7 Place the saucepan or casserole into a warming drawer or oven pre-heated to its very lowest setting. This should be no lower than 175°F/80°C and no higher than 210°F/100°C (about Gas ⅛). You can serve the rice at once, but the longer you leave it, the more separate the grains will be. An hour is fine, but it will be quite safe and happy left for several hours.

Flavouring Rice

The two basic methods of cooking rice just described produce 'plain' or unflavoured rice. Plain rice is perfectly acceptable to eat just as it is. Sometimes it is preferable, when the accompanying dishes are particularly rich. However, plain rice can be considerably enhanced by adding flavourings, which can consist of spices, herbs, onion, garlic, nuts, vegetables, fruit and even flowers.

Some of these flavourings require brief cooking; others do not. They are all best added to the rice after it has itself been cooked.

Opposite, dishes from *Afghanistan* Top to bottom: Lavash bread (page 141), Samboosay (page 172), Boolani Gadana (pages 70–1), Maushawa (page 100), Q'root in the small central pot (page 59), Sabzi Rawash (page 76)

Facing page 129, dishes from *Burma* Top to bottom: Peeteepeepowk Net Shwe (page 96), some gourds, Tha Nat in the coconut (page 167), Ghaw be Thot (page 78), Onon Hitamin (page 137), Swinamakin (page 175)

Norinji Pullao

Rice Flavoured with Orange and Nuts

This absolutely delightful fruit-and-nut rice comes from Afghanistan, which itself shares a border with Iran. The concept of sweet fruit and nuts in tandem with savoury items originates from Persia (Iran), and this Afghan variation produces a very fine rice dish full of contrasting tastes. The recipe includes oranges, pistachios and almonds and is enhanced with onion, brown sugar, aromatic spices and rose water. Any type of orange can be used but, for flavour, clementines or satsumas are perfect.

SERVES: 4   [V]

8–12 oz (225–350 g) basmati rice
2 tablespoons vegetable ghee
2 oz (50 g) onion, finely chopped
15–20 raw pistachio nuts, shelled and whole
15–20 raw almonds, shelled and whole
about 16 orange segments, cut into halves

1–2 teaspoons brown sugar
10–15 saffron stamens
sprinkling of salt (optional)
few drops rose water

Spices
2 inch (5 cm) piece cassia bark
½ teaspoon green cardamom seeds
¼ teaspoon black cummin seeds

1 Prepare and cook the rice by either of the methods explained on pages 126–8.

2 As soon as the rice has begun to boil, heat the ghee in a *karahi* or wok.

3 Stir-fry the **spices** for 30 seconds. Add the onion and stir-fry for a further 3–4 minutes.

4 Add the nuts and stir-fry for a further 3–4 minutes. Take the *karahi* off the heat.

5 The rice will nearly be cooked now, so turn your attention to it until it is cooked to your liking.

6 Drain the boiled rice, shaking off all excess water, and return it to its saucepan (*or* as soon as the rice cooked by absorption is ready, keeping it in its saucepan); add the stir-fry mixture and mix it well into the rice.

7 Add the orange segments, sugar, saffron and optional salt and mix in well. Sprinkle on the rose water.

8 Put the lid on the pan and place it into a warmer or oven preheated to between 175°F/80°C and 210°F/100°C (about Gas ⅛).

9 Leave it there for a minimum of ½ hour, stirring after that time. It can be held in the warmer for longer, if you wish.

Norinji Biriani

This is a variation on the preceding *Norinji Pullao*. A batch of *bhoona* (dry stir-fried curried mixed vegetables) are added to the pullao. Served with a gravy and chutneys the dish becomes a complete meal in its own right.

SERVES: 4   V

1 quantity Norinji Pullao (page 129)
1 lb (450 g) mixed vegetables,
weighed after preparing (equal
quantities of peas, beans, carrots,
potatoes, etc.)

1 tablespoon vegetable ghee
1 tablespoon mild curry paste
½ cupful akhni stock or water
1 tablespoon chopped fresh coriander
leaves

1 First prepare the dry vegetable curry.

2 Cook the vegetables in boiling water until they are as tender as you like them. Drain.

3 Heat the ghee in a *karahi* or wok. Stir-fry the curry paste and the akhni stock or water until it is simmering.

4 Add the vegetables and the fresh coriander and cook until the liquid reduces and the vegetables are quite dry. Remove from the heat.

5 Follow the preceding *Norinji Pullao* recipe from stage 1 to the end of stage 6.

6 Bring the vegetables back to the heat and, when sizzling, add them to the spicy rice.

7 Continue with the *Norinji Pullao* recipe from stage 7 to the end.

Guchi Ka Pullao

Rice Flavoured with Mushrooms or Truffles

I find that mushrooms and rice are highly compatible, especially when a simple aromatic spicing is included. Tiny button mushrooms or the slightly larger cup mushrooms are ideal. But for a special occasion try fresh yellow mushrooms (ceps), a fruity-tasting autumnal variety, or fresh truffles, either white or black. Other alternatives are dried mushrooms. The Chinese dried mushrooms (shiitake) or the dried sponge mushrooms (morel) are excellent in this dish. Both these will need a 4-hour soaking in ample water, then draining, to reconstitute them.

SERVES: 4   V

8–12 oz (225–350 g) basmati rice
2 tablespoons vegetable ghee
2 oz (50 g) onion, finely chopped
about 1 cupful mushrooms or truffles
  of your choice

Spices
1 teaspoon white cummin seeds
½ teaspoon black cummin seeds
¼ teaspoon fennel seeds
1–2 whole star anise

1 Prepare and cook the rice as by either of the methods explained on pages 126–8.

2 As soon as the rice has begun to boil, heat the ghee in a *karahi* or wok.

3 Stir-fry the **spices** for 30 seconds. Add the onion and stir-fry for a further 3–4 minutes.

4 Add the mushrooms or truffles and, when they are sizzling, take them off the heat.

5 Complete the cooking of the rice.

6 Drain the boiled rice, shaking off all excess water and return it to its saucepan (*or* as soon as the rice by absorption is ready, keeping it in its saucepan); add the mushroom or truffle mixture and stir it well into the rice.

7 Put the lid on the pan and place it into a warmer or oven preheated to between 175°F/80°C and 210°F/100°C (about Gas ⅛).

8 Leave it there for a minimum of ½ hour, stirring after that time. It can be held in the warmer for longer, if you wish.

Kashmiri Pullao

Rice Flavoured with Saffron and Nuts

Saffron is the world's most expensive spice. It has no substitute for both flavouring and colouring. But it must be used in the right circumstances so that its delightful properties are enhanced. This rice dish is a perfect vehicle for saffron. You'll know that when you open the pot, just prior to serving. The aroma is divine.

There are four main saffron-growing areas in the world: Spain, Greece, Iran and Kashmir. In the West we mainly use Spanish saffron. In India it is Kashmiri saffron which prevails. There is little difference between them providing that only best-quality saffron is used.

SERVES: 4   V

8–12 oz (225–350 g) basmati rice	*Spices*
2 tablespoons vegetable ghee	*4 green cardamoms*
1 tablespoon ground almonds	*2 inch (5 cm) piece cassia bark*
12–20 saffron stamens	*¼ teaspoon black cummin seeds*

1 Prepare and cook the rice by either of the methods explained on pages 126–8.

2 As soon as the rice has begun to boil, heat the ghee in a *karahi* or wok.

3 Stir-fry the **spices** for 30 seconds. Remove the *karahi* from the heat.

4 Complete the cooking of the rice.

5 Drain the boiled rice, shaking off all excess water, and return it to its saucepan (*or* as soon as the rice cooked by absorption is ready, keeping it in its saucepan); add in the stir-fried spices.

6 Add the ground almonds and the saffron stamens and mix well into the rice.

7 Put the lid on the pan and place it into a warmer or oven pre-heated to between 175°F/80°C and 210°F/100°C (about Gas ⅛).

8 Leave it there for a minimum of ½ hour, stirring after that time. It can be held in the warmer for longer, if you wish.

Brown Rice

This is a Parsee dish and is the natural accompaniment to *dhansak* (page 101). Its name describes the colour of the spicing; not the rice which is traditionally ordinary white basmati rice. You can, of course, use brown basmati rice, and very nice it is too, particularly when spiced this way.

The Curry Club's first gourmet tour to India took place in 1983. I requested a cooking demonstration at our hotel, the Welcom Group's **Searock** (literally sited on rocks at the seaside in a quiet suburb of Bombay). Bombay has a mixture of culinary styles, but the one which fascinated me most is Parsee. We organised a full two-hour Parsee demo, but as the hotel did not at the time have a Parsee chef on the staff, they brought in a lady demonstrator/chef from a company which specialises in cooking the celebrated Parsee wedding feasts, the *lagon nu bhonu*, for as many as 3,000 guests. This is the Parsee Colony's Yezdiar Caterer's recipe for brown rice.

SERVES: 4   [V]

8–12 oz (225–350 g) basmati rice
2 tablespoons vegetable ghee
3 oz (75 g) onion, thinly sliced
2 teaspoons brown sugar
aromatic salt to taste

Spices
1 teaspoon ground cassia
½ teaspoon ground cloves
½ teaspoon green cardamom seeds
¼ teaspoon black cummin seeds

1 Prepare and cook the rice by either of the methods explained on pages 128–8.

2 As soon as the rice has begun to boil, heat the ghee in a *karahi* or wok.

3 Stir-fry the **spices** for 30 seconds. Add the onion and stir-fry for 3–4 minutes. Lower the heat a little, add the sugar and continue to stir-fry until the end of stage 5, by which time the onions should be a lovely golden brown colour.

4 During stage 3, complete the cooking of the rice.

5 Drain the boiled rice, shaking off all excess water, and return it to its saucepan (*or* as soon as the rice cooked by absorption is ready, keeping it in its saucepan); add the stir-fry mixture.

6 Mix in well, adding salt to taste, then put the lid on the pan and place it into a warmer or oven pre-heated to between 175°F/80°C and 210°F/100°C (about Gas ⅛).

7 Leave it there for a minimum of ½ hour, stirring after that time. It can be held in the warmer for longer, if you wish.

Hyderabadi Kabooli

Rice with Chana Dhal

This particular concept, the combination of rice and lentils enhanced by stir-fried flavourings, is a favourite of the former state of Hyderabad, a largely Moslem area, until recently ruled by a fabulously wealthy ruler, the Nizam. This rich dish was frequently served at court as a centre-piece, highly garnished and cooked with meat. I have removed the meat but the decorative garnish remains. It should still be the centre-piece of a meal, served with your choice of accompanying dishes and breads.

SERVES: 4

2 oz (50 g) chana dhal
8–12 oz (225–350 g) basmati rice
2 tablespoons butter ghee
1–2 cloves garlic, finely chopped
1 inch (2·5 cm) cube fresh ginger,
* finely chopped*
2 oz (50 g) onion, thinly sliced
10–12 cashew nuts, shelled and raw
1–2 fresh chillies, finely chopped
* (optional)*
2 tablespoons yoghurt
1 tablespoon finely chopped fresh or 1
* teaspoon dried mint*
1 tablespoon finely chopped fresh
* coriander leaves*
aromatic salt to taste

Spices
1 teaspoon coriander seeds
3 or 4 cloves
2 inch (5 cm) piece cassia bark
2 or 3 whole brown/black cardamoms
½ teaspoon turmeric

Garnish
slices of hard-boiled quail egg
slices of onion tarka (page 38)
10–15 whole almonds, fried
* (optional)*
some whole fresh coriander leaves

1 Pick through the chana dhal to remove any grit or impurities, then soak it for a couple of hours in ample water.

2 Drain, then boil in ample water for about 30 minutes. Drain and keep warm.

3 Prepare and cook the rice by either of the methods explained on pages 126–8.

4 As soon as the rice has begun to boil, heat the ghee in a *karahi* or wok. Stir-fry the **spices** for 30 seconds, then add the garlic and stir-fry for a further minute. Add the ginger and stir-fry for a minute more. Add the onion and stir-fry for about 4 minutes.

5 Add the cashews and the optional chillies and, when sizzling, remove from the heat.

6 Complete the cooking of the rice.

7 Drain the boiled rice, shaking off all excess water, and return it to its saucepan (*or* as soon as the rice cooked by absorption is ready, keeping it in its saucepan); add the stir-fry mixture, the chana, yoghurt, mint, fresh coriander and salt to taste. Mix it all in well.

8 Put the lid on the pan and place it into a warmer or oven pre-heated to between 175°F/80°C and 210°F/100°C (about Gas $\frac{1}{8}$).

9 Leave it there for a minimum of $\frac{1}{2}$ hour, stirring after that time. It can be held in the warmer for longer, if you wish.

10 Place in a serving bowl and decorate with the garnish ingredients.

Thashikasharam

Rice with Lentils, Nuts, Chilli and Lime

I first encountered this traditional South Indian rice dish on a visit to the area. Its distinction is the contrast between the fluffy rice and the crunchy fried lentils and nuts. The flavouring is typical of the region, especially the use of chillies; in South India they would think nothing of putting 20 chillies into this dish! It's up to you if you want plenty of chillies with your rice and lentils or whether you keep them to a minimum, but I recommend that you don't omit them altogether.

SERVES: 4   V

2 tablespoons chana dhal
2 teaspoons polished urid dhal
8–12 oz (225–350 g) basmati rice
2 tablespoons mustard oil
2–4 fresh green chillies, whole
12–15 pre-cooked cashew nuts
1 tablespoon desiccated coconut
juice of 2 limes or 1 lemon
salt to taste

Spices
1 teaspoon mustard seeds
1 teaspoon sesame seeds
$\frac{1}{2}$ teaspoon turmeric
$\frac{1}{8}$ teaspoon asafoetida
6–8 fresh or dried curry leaves

1 Soak the chana and urid dhals for at least 4 hours, then drain for about 1 hour to allow the lentils to dry sufficiently before starting stage 3.

2 Prepare the rice to stage 3 of the boiling method or stage 2 of the absorption method (see pages 126–8).

3 Heat the oil in a *karahi* or wok, and stir-fry the **spices** for about 30 seconds.

4 Add the drained and dried lentils and stir-fry them quite vigorously for about 3 minutes. Add the chillies, then reduce the heat and continue cooking slowly until the lentils become golden and crispy, stirring from time to time. This will take about 10 more minutes. Remove from the heat when you are satisfied, but keep warm.

5 During stage 4, cook the rice as explained on pages 126–8.

6 When it is ready, drain the boiled rice, shaking off all excess water, and return it to its saucepan (*or* as soon as the rice by absorption is ready, keeping it in its saucepan); add the stir-fry mixture, the cashews and coconut and the lime or lemon juice, mixing well. Add salt to taste.

7 Put the lid on the pan and place it into a warmer or oven pre-heated to between 175°F/80°C and 210°F/100°C (about Gas ⅛).

8 Leave it there for a minimum of ½ hour, stirring after that time. It can be held in the warmer for longer, if you wish.

Onon Hitamin

Burmese Coconut Rice

Rice flavoured with coconut will be found in various guises in the southern curry lands, such as South India, Malaya, Indonesia, Thailand and Burma. Fresh coconut would normally be used, the flesh being ground to a paste. It is much easier, however, to use coconut milk powder and it is difficult to tell the difference in the finished dish.

SERVES: 4   V

8–12 oz (225–350 g) basmati rice
2 tablespoons vegetable ghee or
    coconut oil
2 tablespoons coconut milk powder

Spices
½ teaspoon black cummin seeds
½ teaspoon wild onion seeds

1 Prepare and cook the rice by either of the methods explained on pages 126–8.

2 As soon as the rice has begun to boil, heat the ghee or oil in a *karahi* or wok.

3 Stir-fry the **spices** for 30 seconds. Take off the heat, but keep warm.

4 Complete the cooking of the rice.

5 Drain the boiled rice, shaking off all excess water, and return it to its saucepan (*or* as soon as the rice cooked by absorption is ready, keeping it in its saucepan); add the stir-fried spices, stirring in well.

6 Then add the coconut milk powder and mix it in well.

7 Put the lid on the pan and place it into a warmer or oven pre-heated to between 175°F/80°C and 210°F/100°C (about Gas ⅛).

8 Leave it there for a minimum of ½ hour, stirring after that time. It can be held in the warmer for longer, if you wish.

Khao Phed

Thai Red Rice

This is a typical rice dish from Thailand. It has a lovely flavour and goes with any spicy food. It has an underlying red colour, and this is punctuated by the green of the onion and basil and the garnish.

SERVES: 4

8–12 oz (225–350 g) basmati rice
2 tablespoons butter ghee
2 cloves garlic, finely chopped
1 inch (2·5 cm) cube fresh ginger,
  finely chopped
2 oz (50 g) onion, finely chopped
2 eggs
6 spring onion leaves, chopped (the
  bulbs will be used for garnish)
4–6 basil leaves, chopped
1 tablespoon coconut milk powder

2 teaspoons tomato ketchup
1 teaspoon paprika
½–2 teaspoons chilli powder (optional)

Garnish
attractively cut shapes of cucumber
spring onion bulbs, tassels removed
red pepper
whole fresh coriander leaves

1 Prepare and cook the rice by either of the methods on pages 126–8.

2 As soon as the rice has begun to boil, heat the ghee in a *karahi* or wok.

3 Stir-fry the garlic, ginger and onion for 5–6 minutes.

4 Add the eggs and stir-fry vigorously until they scramble and set. Take off the heat. Sprinkle over the spring onion and basil leaves and stir in.

5 Complete the cooking of the rice.

6 Drain the boiled rice, shaking off all excess water, and return it to its saucepan (*or* as soon as the rice cooked by absorption is ready, keeping it in its saucepan); add the stir-fried mixture, the coconut milk powder, tomato ketchup, paprika and optional chilli powder. Mix it all in well.

7 Put the lid on the pan and place into a warmer or oven pre-heated to between 175°F/80°C and 210°F/100°C (about Gas ⅛).

8 Leave it there for a minimum of ½ hour, stirring after that time. It can be held in the warmer for longer, if you wish.

9 When you are ready, place the rice in a serving dish and decorate attractively with the garnish ingredients.

CHAPTER NINE

Breads

All traditional Indian breads are flat discs rolled out from a simple flour and water dough. They are then either dry-cooked on a *tava* (griddle pan), fried, deep-fried or baked in a clay oven. Breads like these have been made in India for millennia.

The most commonly used flour is called *ata* flour, or chupatti flour. This is made from 'hard' wheat grains, finely milled. It is high in gluten and therefore ideal for dough making. *Ata* flour is available in the natural brown form, and a more refined 'white' form (which is in fact a pale buff colour).

Most Indian breads are unleavened, that is to say they contain no raising agent, but they are none the less soft and fluffy. Included and best known in this category is the chupatti, a thin disc about 6 inches (15 cm) in diameter, which is dry-cooked on the *tava*. Also well known is the *paratha*. Here the dough is rolled in layers to create a kind of puff pastry and a disc, thicker and slightly bigger than a chupatti, is rolled out and fried. The *puri* is a small thin disc of about 4 inches (10 cm) in diameter, which is deep-fried and puffs up like a balloon.

One type of Indian bread requires leavening. The naan bread is the tear-drop shaped floppy bread which is cooked in the tandoori oven. The basic dough is given a rising agent (either yeast or yoghurt) and is allowed to rise, which results in even fluffier bread.

In my previous two books (see page 2) I have given recipes for the more common breads, so for this book I have sought out unusual ones from all over India. Some are prepared in an 'unusual' way, whilst others have flavourings incorporated into the actual dough or as toppings. Others use different types of flour such as millet flour, cornflour, rice flour, gram flour or barley flour.

A flip through the following pages will show you just some of the range of unusual possibilities which India has to offer in its range of breads.

Basic Dough Making

Before we get down to the individual breads, it is important to study basic dough making techniques. Once you have mastered the method you will confidently produce perfect bread. The principal secret to success lies in the first kneading, or mixing, of the basic ingredients – flour and water. This requires patient and steady mixing either by hand or by machine, transforming the tacky mass of flour and water into a dough. It should be elastic without being sticky and should feel satisfying to handle. It should also be pliable, springy and soft.

Below are the basic methods for making unleavened and leavened dough.

Unleavened Dough

General Method

flour types and quantities as given in specific recipes

1 Choose a large ceramic or glass bowl and put in the flour.
2 Add water little by little and work it into the flour with your fingers. Soon it will become a lump.
3 Then remove it from the bowl and knead it with your hands on a floured board or work top until the lump is cohesive and well combined.
4 Return it to the bowl and leave it for 10–15 minutes, then briefly knead it once more. It will then be ready to use in the recipes.
5 Use this method in any of the recipes requiring unleavened bread.

Leavened Dough

General Method

flour types and quantities as given in specific recipes
fresh yeast or natural yoghurt

1 Dissolve the fresh yeast in a little lukewarm water.
2 Put the flour in a **warmed** bowl, make a well in the centre and pour in the yeast. Yoghurt can be used in the absence of yeast by non-vegans.
3 Gently mix it into the flour and add enough water to make a firm dough.
4 Remove from the bowl and knead on a floured board until well combined. Return to the bowl and leave in a warm place for a couple of hours to rise.

5 Your dough, when risen, should have doubled in size. It should be bubbly, stringy and elastic.

6 Knock back the dough by kneading it down to its original size.

7 Use this method in any of the following recipes requiring leavened bread.

Lavash

Afghan Flat Leavened Bread

This bread is directly related to both Iranian flat bread and the Indian naan. The shape is an oval of about 8 inches (20 cm) by 4 inches (10 cm).

MAKES: 4 *lavash*   V

2 oz (50 g) fresh yeast or 3 tablespoons
  natural yoghurt
lukewarm water

1½ lb (675 g) white ata (chupatti) flour
1 teaspoon granulated sugar
½ teaspoon salt

1 Using the yeast or yoghurt, water and flour, follow the recipe for leavened dough on page 140, adding the salt and sugar at stage 3 and proceeding through to the end of that recipe.

2 Divide the dough into 4 equal parts.

3 Roll each part into the oval shape described above.

4 Preheat the grill to the three-quarters heat and set the grill pan in the midway position, covering it with foil.

5 Put one *lavash* on to the foil and grill it. Watch it cook (it can *over*cook and burn very easily). As soon as the first side develops brown patches, remove and turn. Repeat until the other side starts to brown.

6 Repeat with the other 3 *lavash*. Serve at once.

Roghni Naan

Spicy Red Leavened Flat Bread

This Kashmiri favourite involves a standard naan bread which is smeared with saffron water and ghee and topped with a spicy tomato and garlic sauce. When grilled it goes a lovely red colour.

MAKES: 4 *roghni naan* **V**

2 oz (50 g) fresh yeast or 3 tablespoons
   natural yoghurt
lukewarm water
1½ lb (675 g) strong white flour
1 tablespoon vegetable oil
1 teaspoon garlic purée
1 teaspoon curry paste
4 canned tomatoes, finely chopped
some saffron water (page 20)
some melted vegetable ghee

Spices
½ teaspoon white poppy seeds
½ teaspoon sesame seeds
¼ teaspoon wild onion seeds

1 Using the yeast, water and white flour, follow the recipe for leavened dough on page 140 to the end of stage 6.

2 Whilst the dough is rising, heat the oil in a *karahi* or wok. Stir-fry the garlic for 1 minute, then add the **spices** and continue for a further minute. Add the curry paste and the tomatoes and stir-fry for a further 10 minutes. Remove from the the heat.

3 Divide the dough into 4 equal parts.

4 Roll each part into a tear-drop shape at least ¼ inch (6 mm) thick.

5 Preheat the grill to three-quarters heat and set the rack pan in the midway position, covering it with foil.

6 Put one naan on to the foil and grill it. Watch it cook (it can easily burn). As soon as the first side develops brown patches, remove it from the grill.

7 Turn it over and brush the uncooked side with the saffron water, then with the melted ghee. Lightly score into the top side with a knife, then spread a thin layer of the stir-fry mixture on it.

8 Return it to the grill and cook until it is sizzling. Remove.

9 Repeat stages 6 to 8 with the other 3 naan. Serve at once.

Khurmee Naan

Leavened Flat Bread Topped with Dates and Jaggery

Also from Kashmiri, this naan bread variant is smeared with a sweet mixture of dates (*khurma*) and jaggery (or *gur*), a sweet molasses-type extract.

MAKES: 4 *khurmee naan*   V

4 roghni naan (opposite)
6–8 soft dates, stoned
1–2 tablespoons jaggery or brown
*   sugar syrup*

1 Follow the preceding recipe to the end of stage 9, omitting stage 2. In place of stage 2, finely chop the dates and mix with brown sugar syrup, or, if you can get it, jaggery.

2 Spread this on the naan in place of the tomato mixture at stage 7.

3 Serve hot and at once.

Roqui Roti

Dough Kneaded with Ghee

This is a thin chupatti-type bread in that it is made from brown *ata* flour and rolled to about 6 inch (15 cm) discs. This version, from Hyderabad, incorporates ghee into the dough, which causes the disc to become quite crisp when cooked.

MAKES: 8 *roqui rotis*　　 V

1 lb (450 g) brown ata or wholemeal
　flour
2 tablespoons melted vegetable ghee

1　Following the recipe for unleavened bread on page 140, mix the flour with water to make the dough.

2　Add the melted ghee and mix it well into the dough.

3　Divide the dough into 8 equal lumps.

4　Shape each lump into a ball, then on a floured work surface roll each ball into a thin disc about 6 inches (15 cm) in diameter.

5　Heat a dry *tava* (griddle pan) or frying pan on medium-high heat, then place a *roqui roti* on the *tava*.

6　Cook it for a minute or so until it starts to brown. Turn it over and cook the other side. Place it in a warming drawer or very low oven.

7　Repeat with the other 7 *roqui rotis*. Serve as hot as possible.

Do-Palli or Do-Pattri

Twin-Layered Chupatti

This bread has a secret which the diner only discovers when it is picked up: it is in fact two chupattis stuck together. The fun is to peel them apart and, hey presto, you have two very thin chupattis!

MAKES: 4 *do-pallis*   [V]

1 lb (450 g) brown ata or wholemeal
* flour*
2–4 tablespoons melted vegetable ghee

1 Following the recipe for unleavened bread on page 140, mix the flour with water to make the dough.

2 Divide the dough into 8 equal lumps.

3 Shape each lump into a ball, then on a floured work surface roll each ball into a thin disc about 3 inches (7·5 cm) in diameter.

4 Brush the melted ghee onto the top surface of the disc, then place another disc exactly on top of the first.

5 Roll this double disc out to about 6 inches (15 cm) in diameter.

6 Repeat stages 4 and 5 to make 3 further *do-pallis*.

7 Heat a *tava* (griddle pan) or frying pan on medium-high heat, then place a *do-palli* on the *tava*.

8 Cook it for a minute or two until it starts to brown. Turn it over and cook the other side. Place it in a warming drawer or a very low oven.

9 Repeat with the other 3 *do-pallis*. Serve as hot as possible.

Rotli

Thin Unleavened Wheat Flour Discs

From Gujarat comes a family of breads called *rotli*. Made from *ata* flour, they are rolled into very thin discs, then dry-griddled. They are like chupattis but much thinner and lighter. A variation includes *dal-dhokli*, where the dough is combined with cooked lentils and the bread is rolled up, cut into pieces, and served with gravy: it is a complete meal in itself. Another variation is *khakra*, which are cooked slowly until they become completely dry. Like biscuits, they stay edible for days. A further variation is called *bhakri*, made from millet (*bajra*) flour (see *Bajra Rotla* on page 152).

MAKES: 8 *rotli*   [V]

*1 lb (450 g) brown ata or wholemeal
flour*

1 Following the recipe for unleavened bread on page 140, mix the flour with water to make the dough.

2 Divide the dough into 8 equal lumps.

3 Shape each lump into a ball, then roll each ball into a disc, literally as thin and as large in diameter as you can.

4 Heat a *tava* (griddle pan) or large frying pan on medium-high heat, then carefully lift a *rotli* and place it on to the *tava*.

5 Cook it for 45 seconds or so, until it starts to fleck with brown. Carefully turn it over and cook the other side.

6 Fold it in half and place in a warming drawer or very low oven.

7 Repeat with the other 7 *rotli* and serve as hot as possible.

Dal-Dhokli   [V]

Thin Unleavened Wheat Flour and Lentil Discs

1 To make *dal-dhokli*, add 4–6 tablespoons of (cold) cooked lentils to the dough during stage 1 of the previous recipe.

2 Follow that recipe to the end to make 8 *dal-dhoklis*. Roll each *dal-dhoklis* up, slice into pieces and serve with curry masala gravy.

Khakra [V]

Thin Unleavened Wheat Flour Crispy Discs

1 To make *khakra*, follow the recipe for *rotli* through to the end of stage 5.

2 Then place the *rotlis* into the oven preheated to 300°F/150°C/Gas 2 and bake them until they go quite hard and crispy (about 10 minutes). Serve hot or cold. They will keep, like biscuits, broken up in an airtight tin.

Phulka

Double-Cooked Chupatti

This bread is in fact nothing more than a thick chupatti. It is dry-cooked to start with, then it is held directly over a naked flame and instantly browns and puffs up.

MAKES: 4 *phulka*   [V]

*1 lb (450 g) brown ata or wholemeal
  flour*

1 Following the recipe for unleavened bread on page 140, mix the flour with water to make the dough.

2 Divide the dough into 4 equal lumps.

3 Shape each lump into a ball, then roll each ball into a disc about 6 inches (15 cm) in diameter.

4 Heat a *tava* (griddle pan) or large frying pan on a high heat. Place a *phulka* on to the *tava*.

5 Cook it for a minute or more, until it is evenly cooked and starts to fleck with brown. Turn it over and do the same with the other side.

6 Remove the *tava* from the heat, then dab the *phulka* directly on to the flame. (It works best with gas, but acceptably with electric rings. It does not work with ceramic rings.) It will at once puff up and blacken at the point where it is dabbed. Continue quick dabs until you are satisfied. Place the *phulka* into a warming drawer or very low oven.

7 Repeat with the other 3 *phulka*. Serve as hot as possible.

Lachadar Paratha

Rope-Dough Layered Fried Bread

Like all *paratha*, this one is rolled into layers, then fried. But unlike other *paratha*, the layers are ribbon-like and very loose so that, whilst being flaky, it has a unique texture.

MAKES: 4 *lachadar paratha*   [V]

1 lb (450 g) brown ata or wholemeal
*   flour*
4 tablespoons melted vegetable ghee
further melted vegetable ghee

1 Following the recipe for unleavened bread on page 140, mix the flour with water to make the dough.

2 Add the melted ghee and mix well into the dough.

3 Divide the dough into 4 equal lumps.

4 Shape the first lump into a long sausage, then flatten it into a strip about 12 by 3 inches (30 by 7·5 cm).

5 Apply further melted ghee to the strip, then roll it from the long side to make a 'snake'.

6 Gently flatten the snake with a rolling pin back into a strip of the same dimension as above. You now have layered dough.

7 Cut the strip into 2 strips about 12 by 1½ inches (30 by 3·75 cm).

8 Now coil one strip around itself into a shape like a three-dimensional ice cream cone.

9 Lightly press it down with your hand, brush it with ghee and coil the second strip on top in the same shape.

10 Sprinkle extra flour on to the cone and again lightly press it down, then very lightly roll it out to a disc about 7 inches (17·5 cm) in diameter. It should be obviously flaky and layered.

11 Heat a further 2 tablespoons of ghee on a *tava* (griddle pan) or large frying pan and fry the *paratha* until it is hot. Lift it out with tongs. Add more ghee and repeat on the other side. Keep in a warming drawer or very low oven.

12 Repeat stages 4 to 11 to make the remaining 3 *parathas*. Serve as hot and fresh as possible.

Bathuway Ka Roti

Spinach Paratha

This is a spicy Punjabi bread. The dough mixture is kneaded with spinach and spices. It is then rolled in layers and fried.

MAKES: 4 *bathuway ka roti*   V

1 lb (450 g) brown ata or wholemeal flour
2 tablespoons melted vegetable ghee
4 tablespoons spinach leaves, chopped, blanched, drained and cooled
1 tablespoon chopped fresh coriander leaves

1 teaspoon cummin seeds, roasted
½ teaspoon dried fenugreek leaves
½ teaspoon salt (optional)
further melted vegetable ghee

1 Follow stages 1 and 2 of the previous (*lachadar paratha*) recipe, adding the spinach, coriander leaves, cummin, fenugreek and optional salt at stage 2.

2 Follow stages 3, 4 and 5 of the previous recipe. Omit stages 6 and 7.

3 Coil one snake into a shape like a three-dimensional ice cream cone.

4 Sprinkle extra flour on to the cone and lightly press it down with your hand, then very lightly roll it out to a disc about 8 inches (20 cm) in diameter. It should be nicely layered.

5 Follow stage 11 of the previous recipe.

6 Repeat to make the remaining 3 *parathas*. Serve as hot and fresh as possible.

Tikker

Wheat and Cornflour Bread, Topped with Onion, Garlic, Tomato, Chilli and Coriander

The best way to envisage this rather excellent bread from Rajasthan is to call it a pizza. It is cooked by dry-griddling and finished under the grill. Make the filling first, or while the dough is rising.

MAKES: 4 *tikkers*   [V]

The Filling
2 tablespoons vegetable ghee
2–4 cloves garlic, thinly sliced
2 oz (50 g) onion, finely sliced
½ teaspoon ground coriander
½ teaspoon ground cummin
½ teaspoon garam masala
2 or 3 tomatoes, finely chopped
1–2 fresh green chillies, sliced
½ tablespoon chopped fresh coriander
   leaves
aromatic salt to taste

The Dough
2 oz (50 g) fresh yeast or 3 tablespoons
   natural yoghurt
12 oz (350 g) brown ata or wholemeal
   flour
4 oz (110 g) corn flour

The Filling

1 Heat the ghee in a *karahi* or wok. Stir-fry the garlic for 1 minute; add the onion and stir-fry for a couple more minutes.

2 Add the coriander, cummin and garam masala and stir-fry for a further minute or so.

3 Add the remaining filling ingredients, and stir-fry for about 5 minutes. Allow to cool.

The Dough

4 Following the recipe for unleavened bread on page 140, mix the yeast and the flours with water to make the dough.

5 Divide the dough into 4 equal-sized lumps.

6 Shape the first lump into a ball, then on a floured work surface roll it out to a disc about 6 inches (15 cm) in diameter.

7 Heat a *tava* (griddle pan) or frying pan on a medium-high heat.

8 Place the *tikker* on to the *tava* and cook it for about 2 minutes. Remove.

9 Press down the top side to create a saucer-like depression, then spread an even layer of filling into the depression.

10 Put some foil on the grill pan and place the *tikker* on to it. Put the pan into the midway position of the grill, preheated to medium heat.

11 Cook for a minute or so, until the filling sizzles and the edges begin to blacken. Keep in a warming drawer or very low oven.

12 Repeat stage 6 to 11 to make the other 3 *tikkers*.

13 Serve hot as a snack or to accompany a main-course meal.

Note: Freeze any spare filling.

Bajra Rotla

Millet Flour Discs, Decorated with Finger Prints

This bread is a Gujarati speciality. The dough is made from millet flour and is rolled out into a thick disc. This is decorated with a series of depressions made with the finger tips and is then baked. A variation in shape is called *batlou*. *Debra* is another variation, where spinach and chilli are incorporated into the dough. Instructions for making *batlou* and *debra* follow.

MAKES: 4 *bajra rotlas*   V

1 lb (450 g) millet flour

1 Following the recipe for unleavened bread on page 140, mix the flour with water to make the dough.

2 Divide the dough into 4 equal-sized lumps.

3 Shape each lump into a ball.

4 On a floured work surface, roll the first ball into a disc about 5 inches (12·5 cm) in diameter.

5 With the tip of your forefinger, make a series of small depressions all over the *bajra rotla*.

6 Repeat stages 4 and 5 to make the other *bajra rotlas*.

7 Put foil onto the grill pan, then place 2 *bajra rotlas* on to the foil. Put the pan into the midway position of the grill, preheated to medium heat, and cook for 1–2 minutes, watching that they do not burn.

8 Turn them over and repeat. Keep them in a warming drawer or very low oven.

9 Repeat stages 7 and 8 to cook the other 2 *bajra rotlas*. Serve hot.

Batlou   V

To make 4 *batlous*, follow the recipe above exactly. Simply make the *batlous* square instead of round.

Debra   V

To make 4 *debras*, follow the recipe for *bajra rotla*. Add exactly the same extra ingredients as given in the *bathuway ka roti* recipe on page 149.

Podi Pathir

Rice Flour Chupatti

This is best described as a chupatti, in that it is a thin disc rolled out to about 6 inches (15 cm) in diameter. The difference is that its dough is made from rice flour, giving it a startling white appearance. The *podi pathir* is a speciality of the small Moslem community from Malabar in South India.

MAKES: 8 *podi pathirs*   V

1 lb (450 g) rice flour

1 Following the recipe for unleavened bread on page 140, mix the flour with water to make the dough.

2 Divide the dough into 8 equal lumps.

3 Shape each lump into a ball, then on a rice-floured work surface roll each ball into a thin disc about 6 inches (15 cm) in diameter.

4 Heat a dry *tava* (griddle pan) or frying pan on medium-high heat, then place a *podi pathir* on the *tava*.

5 Cook it for a minute or so until it starts to fleck with brown. Turn it over and cook the other side. Place it in a warming drawer or very low oven.

6 Repeat with the other 7 *podi pathirs*. Serve as hot as possible.

Koda Roti

Barley Flour Bread

This bread is enjoyed in the Himalayas. It is like a chupatti, being dry-cooked, but the flour is barley flour, giving it a distinctive flavour.

MAKES: 8 *koda roti*   V

1 lb (450 g) barley flour

Follow the previous *Podi Pathir* recipe exactly, using barley flour instead of rice flour.

Radha Bollobi

Gram Flour Puri

The *puri* is a small disc, about 3 to 4 inches (7·5 to 10 cm) in diameter, which is deep-fried and puffs up into a crispy balloon. This Bengali version uses gram flour to achieve the same effect and a distinctive flavour.

MAKES: 16 *radha bollobis*   [V]

8 oz (225 g) gram flour
1 teaspoon sugar
½ teaspoon aromatic salt

1 Following the recipe for unleavened bread on page 140, mix the flour with water to make the dough, adding the sugar and salt at an early stage.

2 Divide the dough into 4 equal lumps and divide each lump into 4, to get 16 small equal-sized lumps.

3 Shape each lump into a ball, then on a gram-floured work surface roll each ball into a small thin disc about 3½ inches (7·75 cm) in diameter.

4 Heat the deep-fryer to 375°F/190°C and immerse one disc in the oil. It will sink initially, then rise and, hopefully, puff up like a balloon. Turn it when it does this and remove after 30 seconds or so, when it should be golden. Shake off excess oil and keep the *puri* in a warming drawer or very low oven.

5 Repeat with the remaining *puris*. Serve as hot and fresh as possible.

· CHAPTER TEN ·

Chutneys and Pickles

Chutneys and pickles are an indispensable accompaniment to the curry meal. They are to be found all over the curry lands. Some are uncooked, requiring virtually no time to prepare, and are served at once. Others require long cooking and weeks to mature. Some are savoury and others are sweet. They are all delicious and appetising and make rich curry and spicy dishes that bit more interesting. Indeed, some of the people of the curry lands look forward to their accompaniments so much that they claim to enjoy them even more than the main dishes! I am not sure that I can carry my own enthusiasm to that extreme, but I must say that I could not contemplate eating a curry meal without a good selection of chutneys and pickles.

In this chapter I have drawn on a wealth of material from countries as far apart as Afghanistan and Indonesia, Nepal and Sri Lanka, to bring you as wide a selection of accompaniments as possible. I can testify that each recipe is perfectly suited to accompany any of the main dishes in this book. I hope that in time you will work through them all and prove me right!

Shaftalu

Peach Chutney

This sweet and savoury chutney from Afghanistan is cooked, then chilled.

MAKES: enough for 4   V

1 tablespoon mustard oil
1 tablespoon tamarind purée or
  vinegar (any type)
2 ripe peaches and 1 tablespoon brown
  sugar or 2 canned peaches and 1
  tablespoon of their syrup
aromatic salt to taste

Spices
$\frac{1}{4}$ *teaspoon black cummin seeds*
$\frac{1}{4}$ *teaspoon chilli powder*
$\frac{1}{4}$ *teaspoon fennel seeds*

1 Heat the oil in a *karahi* or wok. Stir-fry the **spices** for 1 minute, then add the tamarind or vinegar.

2 As soon as it simmers, add the peaches and sugar or canned peaches and syrup.

3 Take off the heat and add salt to taste. When cool, chill in the refrigerator. Serve cold when wanted.

Arkrhot

Walnut, Chilli and Yoghurt Chutney

This is a fine chutney from Kashmir where, unlike much of India, walnuts prevail. The Kashmiris grind the ingredients into a paste, but I prefer to keep the nuts chunky. It is normally quite chilli-hot, but by omitting the chillies it becomes very mild.

MAKES: enough for 4

12–15 walnuts
0–6 fresh red chillies (optional)
½ teaspoon ground cassia

½ teaspoon aromatic salt
4 fl oz (120 ml) thick (Greek) natural
*   yoghurt*

1 Shell the walnuts and chop them coarsely.

2 Finely chop the optional chillies.

3 Combine all the ingredients, mixing well.

4 Place them in a serving bowl and put it into the fridge. Serve when cold. Being yoghurt based, this chutney will keep for several days.

Gasneech

Fresh Coriander and Walnut Chutney

Walnuts are popular in this Afghan recipe, which contrasts interestingly with the previous *arkrhot* recipe.

MAKES: enough for 4   V

6 tablespoons coarsely chopped fresh
*   coriander leaves*
2–4 cloves garlic
2 oz (50 g) onion, coarsely chopped

4 tablespoons sugar
2 teaspoons aromatic salt
20 shelled walnuts

1 Combine everything except the walnuts in an electric blender or food processor and grind to a purée, adding enough water to obtain a thick porridge-like consistency.

2 Quarter the walnuts and mix them in. Keep in the fridge and use within 2 days.

Tursho Peyaz

Vinegared Onion Rings

Tursho (vinegared pickles) are very popular in Iran and the Middle East. This simple version is popular in Afghanistan, using onion (*peyaz*). The concept of *tursho* does not seem to have travelled further east into India. I know not why, because this chutney goes well with all curry dishes.

MAKES: enough for 4   V

*1 large Spanish onion (about
    8 oz/225 g)
1 teacup white spirit vinegar*

*½ teaspoon garlic purée
1 teaspoon sugar*

1 Choose a large healthy onion. Peel it and thinly slice it all the way across into rings.

2 Break out as many rings as you can. Use unsatisfactory parts for something else.

3 Mix the vinegar, garlic and sugar in a bowl and immerse the rings in the mixture for at least 6 hours in the refrigerator.

4 Serve when ready.

Chaat

Fresh Vegetable and Fruit Chutney

Fresh raw crunchy vegetables and fruit are spiced and served cold in this tangy Pakistani chutney. The vegetable and fruit used is your own choice. Here is an example:

MAKES: enough for 4   V

2 or 3 sticks celery
4 inch (10 cm) piece cucumber
½ red pepper
1–2 fresh green chillies (optional)
1 small stick rhubarb
1 small cooking apple
8 white cherries
4 gooseberries
1 tangerine

juice of one lemon
aromatic salt to taste

Spices
½ teaspoon ground coriander
½ teaspoon ground cummin
½ teaspoon mango powder
¼ teaspoon ground black pepper

1 Wash all the vegetables and fruit.

2 Dice the celery, cucumber, red pepper, optional chillies, rhubarb and apple into about ¼ inch (6 mm) cubes.

3 Stone and quarter the cherries; quarter the gooseberries; peel the tangerine and quarter the segments.

4 Mix all the above ingredients together with the **spices**, lemon juice and salt to taste.

5 Put the *chaat* into a serving bowl and chill in the refrigerator, serving within ½ hour.

Garjar Am

Shredded Carrot with Mango

This is a simple and effective Gujarati chutney, combining sour and sweet tastes.

MAKES: enough for 4   V

3 or 4 large carrots
flesh of $\frac{1}{2}$ mango, chopped
2 tablespoons tamarind purée
juice of 1 lemon

$\frac{1}{2}$ teaspoon mustard seeds
1–2 tablespoons brown sugar
aromatic salt to taste

1 Wash and scrape the carrots, then shred them using a grater or a food processor.

2 Mix the remaining ingredients together, adding enough water to make a runny liquid mixture.

3 Combine it with the carrots, mixing well so that all the carrot is covered with the liquid. Add salt to taste.

4 Place in a serving bowl and put in the refrigerator for at least 6 hours (maximum 24 hours).

5 Serve when ready.

Dishes from *Gujarat and Central India*   Clockwise from top: brass discs and ompadi press with a selection of crunchy nibbles (page 40–5), Hyderabadi Kabooli (page 134), Kachu Paka (page 63) with Rotli bread (page 146), Chaat Paapri Ke Gol Goppa served with Jal Jeera drink in the brass beaker (page 56)

Kosumbri

—————◆—————

Carrot and Coconut Chutney

Kosumbri simply means spiced raw salad and it is popular in South India. Traditionally lentils are used, but in this quick version carrot is the principal ingredient.

MAKES: enough for 4   V

3 or 4 large carrots
2 tablespoons mustard oil
1 teaspoon mustard seeds
1 teaspoon grated or desiccated
  coconut

0–4 fresh red chillies (optional)
juice of 1 lemon
salt to taste

1 Wash and scrape the carrots, then cut them into julienne strips (matchsticks).

2 Heat the oil in a *karahi* or wok. Stir-fry the mustard seeds for 30 seconds, then add the coconut, optional chillies and lemon juice.

3 Stir-fry this mixture for 3–4 minutes, then remove from the heat. Add the carrot and mix in well. Allow to cool.

4 Add salt to taste. Place in a serving bowl and chill in the refrigerator for at least 6 hours (maximum 24 hours).

5 Serve when ready.

Dishes from *Sri Lanka and South India*   Top to bottom: Sri Lankan Fantasy (page 174), a selection of chillies and fresh pepper on the vine, Laala Phalia Ka Til Salat (page 65), Papadoms (page 46). On the thali tray, clockwise from top: Sev (pages 40–1), Thoran (page 80), plain rice (pages 126–8) Philourie (pages 68–9), Anasi Mallung (page 165) Kosumbri (above) and Imasha in the centre (page 84)

Urugai

Gooseberry Pickle

Hot sour pickles (*urugai*) are extremely popular in southern India. Mango, lime and chilli are the best known, but gooseberries are also excellent for pickling. This recipe involves a relatively long process as the finished pickle should be allowed to mature in an ample quantity of oil for a few weeks before it is used. Consequently, this recipe makes enough pickle for many helpings.

MAKES: enough for many helpings   V

2 lb 3 oz (1 kg) gooseberries
1 tablespoon salt
6 fl oz (175 ml) vegetable oil
1 tablespoon mustard seeds

6–10 cloves garlic, finely chopped
8 oz (225 g) onion purée
4 tablespoons mild curry paste

1 Wash the gooseberries and remove the stalks. Blanch them in boiling water for 3–4 minutes.

2 Drain them, sprinkle with the salt and leave them, covered, overnight.

3 Next day, heat the oil in a *karahi* or wok. Stir-fry the mustard seeds for 30 seconds.

4 Add the garlic and stir-fry for a further 2 minutes. Add the onion purée and the curry paste and stir-fry this mixture for about 10 minutes.

5 Add the gooseberries to the *karahi*, bring to a simmer and stir-fry for about 5 minutes. Remove from the heat and allow to cool.

6 Wash some jam jars and dry them thoroughly in a warming drawer or very low oven.

7 When the pickle is cool enough, transfer it to the jars, filling them to the top and ensuring that there is sufficient oil in each jar. Cap the jars and shake the pickle down.

8 Inspect the jars after a couple of days, ensuring that there is at least $\frac{1}{2}$ inch (1·25 cm) oil above the pickle to prevent it moulding on top. If not, heat some more oil and pour in.

9 Leave for at least a month before serving.

Tamako Achar

Bamboo Shoot Pickle

Nepal is home to bamboo. It grows prolifically all over the country, and especially in Kathmandu where this recipe comes from. This is an oil-based pickle requiring a relatively long cooking time, followed by a long maturation in bottles, so this recipe makes a largish batch. Although the Nepalese use fresh shoots, I find that canned sliced bamboo shoots are ideal for this recipe.

MAKES: enough for many helpings   V

2 lb 3 oz (1 kg) canned sliced bamboo
  shoots (weighed after draining)
1 tablespoon salt
6 fl oz (175 ml) vegetable oil

6–10 cloves garlic, finely chopped
8 oz (225 g) onion purée
4 tablespoons mild curry paste

1   Drain the canned bamboo shoots (use the liquid for stock in another recipe).

2   Heat the oil in a *karahi* or wok.

3   Follow stages 4 to 9 of the previous (*urugai*) recipe, substituting the bamboo shoots for the gooseberries, and adding the salt at the end of stage 4.

Hoopoo

Coconut Chutney

A simple and tasty chutney from South India, served cold.

MAKES: enough for 4   V

flesh of ½ coconut and its water
1 teaspoon mustard seeds
0–1 teaspoons chilli powder
  (optional)

1 tablespoon chopped fresh coriander
  leaves
salt to taste

1 Grate the coconut as finely as you can.

2 Spread it on an oven pan and sprinkle on the mustard seeds. Grill at medium heat with the pan in the midway position for less than a minute. Watch that it does not burn.

3 Mix the above in a bowl with the coconut water and the other ingredients.

4 Transfer to a serving bowl and chill in the refrigerator for an hour or so. Serve when ready.

Mooli Chatni

White Radish Chutney

I encountered this recipe in Bombay. It works especially well with mooli, which has a slightly peppery taste.

MAKES: enough for 4   V

6 inch (15 cm) piece mooli (white
  radish)
1 teaspoon mild curry paste
3 fl oz (85 ml) vinegar (any type)

1 teaspoon tomato paste
1 teaspoon tamarind purée
1 teaspoon brown sugar
salt to taste

1 Shred the mooli using a grater or a food processor.

2 Mix the curry paste with the vinegar, tomato paste, tamarind purée, sugar and salt to taste.

3 Combine with the mooli.

4 Place in a serving bowl and chill in the refrigerator for a minimum of 6 hours (maximum 24 hours). Serve when ready.

Anasi Mallung

Pineapple Chutney

The *mallung* is a mixed vegetable dish from Sri Lanka. This particular *mallung* uses pineapple mixed with coconut and in this instance is served cold as a chutney.

MAKES: enough for 4　　V

½ *pineapple*
2 tablespoons mustard oil
1 teaspoon mustard seeds
3 tablespoons desiccated coconut

½ *teaspoon turmeric*
0–2 teaspoons chilli powder
　(optional)
salt to taste

1 Cut the outer scales off the pineapple, coring the remnants as necessary. Cut the soft flesh into about ⅓ inch (8 mm) cubes.

2 Heat the oil in a *karahi* or wok and stir-fry the mustard seeds for 30 seconds, then add the coconut, turmeric and optional chilli powder and stir-fry for a further 2–3 minutes.

3 Add the pineapple and mix well. Remove from the heat and add salt to taste.

4 When cold, transfer to a serving bowl and place in the refrigerator for 1–2 hours. Serve when ready.

Nam Prik

Thai Hot Chilli Sauce

Literally meaning hot (*prik*) liquid (*nam*), this is the celebrated heat agent which accompanies Thai food. This sauce goes well with any dish, providing you enjoy heat.

MAKES: enough for several helpings [V]

12 fresh red chillies, chopped
1 red capsicum pepper, chopped
6 cloves garlic
1 tablespoon brown sugar

4 fl oz (100 ml) lemon juice (bottled
  or fresh)
2 fl oz (50 ml) vinegar (any type)
4 teaspoons chilli powder

1 Grind everything by hand or in a food processor to obtain a thickish but runny purée. Add water to get the final consistency to your liking.

2 Serve cold. It will keep in the fridge for several days.

Sambal Oelek

Indonesian Hot Chilli Sauce

Indonesians enjoy very hot food and this condiment (*sambal*) is indeed very hot. It goes well with any of the dishes in this book – providing, of course, you like hot things.

MAKES: enough for several helpings [V]

15–20 fresh red chillies, chopped
1 tablespoon extra-hot chilli powder
2 tablespoons tamarind purée

3 fl oz (75 ml) vinegar (any type)
1 tablespoon brown sugar
1 teaspoon soy sauce (kecap manis)

Follow the method for the previous (*nam prik*) recipe.

Taeng Kwah Yam

Cucumber Chutney

From Thailand comes this simple sweet-and-sour accompaniment.

MAKES: enough for 4   V

6 inch (15 cm) piece cucumber
2 oz (50 g) onion, thinly sliced
2 fl oz (50 ml) vinegar (any type)
1 tablespoon tamarind purée
1 teaspoon soy sauce

2 teaspoons brown sugar
0–2 teaspoons chilli powder
   (optional)
salt to taste

1 Peel the cucumber, discarding the skin. Dice into $\frac{1}{4}$ inch (6 mm) cubes.

2 Mix the remaining ingredients together, then add the cucumber.

3 Place the mixture in a serving bowl and put in the refrigerator for a minimum of 6 hours (maximum 24 hours) to marinate. Serve when ready.

Tha Nat

Cucumber Chutney

The Burmese also have a classic cucumber chutney recipe, which makes an interesting contrast with the previous Thai one.

MAKES: enough for 4   V

6 inch (15 cm) piece cucumber
2 tablespoons sesame oil
1 teaspoon sesame seeds
1 teaspoon garlic, finely chopped

1 tablespoon onion, finely chopped
4 fl oz (100 ml) vinegar (any type)
$\frac{1}{2}$ teaspoon sugar
salt to taste

1 Cut the cucumber into thick julienne strips (matchsticks).

2 Heat the oil in a *karahi* or wok. Stir-fry the sesame seeds for 30 seconds. Add the garlic and stir-fry for 2 minutes. Add the onion and stir-fry for a further 2 minutes.

3 Add the vinegar and, when simmering, add the cucumber. Stir-fry for about 5 minutes, then remove from the heat.

4 Add the sugar and salt. When cold, place in a serving bowl and put in the refrigerator for an hour or two. Serve when ready.

Sauos Kachang

Peanut Sauce

This peanut sauce is from Indonesia. It has many uses including as a flavouring in cooking or to coat items for satay. Equally, it makes an excellent chutney.

MAKES: enough for several helpings   [V]

7 oz (200 g) raw peanuts
4 tablespoons sunflower or light oil
2 teaspoons garlic purée
2 oz (50 g) onion purée
0–2 teaspoons chilli powder
  (optional)
1 tablespoon tomato ketchup
1 tablespoon lemon juice (fresh or
  bottled)

3 tablespoons vinegar (any type)
1 tablespoon brown sugar
1 tablespoon soy sauce (kecap manis)
1 tablespoon peanut butter
salt to taste

1 Spread the peanuts on an oven tray. Place it at the midway position under a grill at medium heat. Grill for 3–4 minutes, avoiding burning. Allow to cool, then grind with enough water to make a paste either by hand or in a food processor.

2 Heat the oil in a *karahi* or wok. Stir-fry the garlic and onion purées for about 5 minutes. Add the remaining ingredients, including the peanut paste, and stir-fry for 10–15 minutes on a low to medium heat.

3 Allow to cool, then bottle and use as required. Keep the bottle in the refrigerator, where it will be safe for a few days.

Buah Tomat

Tomato Chutney

From Malaya comes this rather nice red tomato chutney. The chilli powder can be omitted if you wish to avoid heat.

MAKES: enough for several helpings   [V]

4 tablespoons sunflower or light oil
4 oz (110 g) onion purée
4–6 canned tomatoes
1 teaspoon brown sugar

1 tablespoon tomato ketchup
1 tablespoon tomato paste
0–2 teaspoons chilli powder (optional)
salt to taste

1 Heat the oil in a *karahi* or wok. Stir-fry the onion purée for 5–8 minutes.

2 Drain the canned tomatoes (use the juice for something else) and mash them up.

3 Add them to the *karahi* with all the other ingredients. When it bubbles, reduce the heat to medium and simmer for about 15 minutes, stirring from time to time.

4 Remove from the heat and, when cool, place in a serving bowl and chill in the refrigerator, where it will keep safely for several days. Serve when ready.

Achar Kunning

Pickled Vegetables

This final accompaniment recipe also comes from Malaya. It is a cooked vinegar-based chutney, using vegetables of your choice. Its acidity is tempered by a little sugar, but it is designed to compliment rich curry dishes with its contrast in taste. It should keep indefinitely, so this recipe makes a reasonable quantity.

MAKES: enough for many helpings   [V]

Suggested vegetables
3 or 4 large carrots
1 small cauliflower
8 oz (225 g) bean sprouts
3 or 4 sticks celery
2–4 chillies, whole
3 tablespoons sunflower or light oil

4 cloves garlic, finely sliced
8 oz (225 g) onion, finely sliced
½ teaspoon turmeric
2 oz (50 g) raw peanuts, chopped
1 pint (600 ml) distilled white vinegar
2 teaspoons salt

1 Prepare the suggested vegetables or vegetables of your choice, dicing them into small bite-sized pieces.

2 Heat the oil in a *karahi* or wok. Stir-fry the garlic for 2 minutes. Add the onion and continue stir-frying for 3–4 minutes more. Add the turmeric and stir in the chopped peanuts. Remove from the heat.

3 Add the vinegar, salt and diced vegetables, and mix in well.

4 Put into clean dry jars, ensuring that the vinegar covers the contents to the top of the jar. Jiggle the jar to dislodge bubbles, topping up if needed. Cap the jar and store away.

5 Inspect after a couple of days. Top up with vinegar if needed.

6 Leave for at least 2 weeks to mature.

CHAPTER ELEVEN

Desserts and Sweet Things

I have to say that, without exception, the peoples of the curry lands have a really sweet tooth. Also their range of dessert recipes is strictly limited. Pies and flans containing fruit and light cakes and gâteaux are unknown. This is not to say that their puddings are boring. Far from it. Much use is made of sugar, syrup and dairy products and of course fruit of every type abounds and appears at every meal.

I have considerably reduced the sugar content in this small selection of recipes. (You can of course add more.) Otherwise they are a representative selection from the curry countries.

From Afghanistan in the west is the *samboosay*, a triangular pastry of the samosa family with a sweet filling. From India I have chosen a light mango syllabub, whilst from Sri-Lanka is a fruit salad laced with alcohol. An interesting recipe from Burma uses semolina to create either a hot runny pudding or a cold fudge as the mood takes you. From Thailand comes sticky sweet rice balls and from our most easterly 'curry land', Indonesia, is one of the most popular puddings, banana fritters. I'm sure you'll find something to your liking here, and that you'll enjoy these distinctive desserts suitable for rounding off a curry meal.

Samboosay

Sweet Samosa

The *samboosay* is a speciality from Afghanistan. It is an absolute delight. So much so that it can be eaten at any time of the day served hot or cold – try it at breakfast for a real change, or at tea time. It also makes a splendid pudding, when it can be enhanced with cream and/or syrup.

To make the *samboosay* casing, follow the pastry and folding instructions on page 74. In this example I have used apples for the filling, but you can use any fruit you like. This recipe makes 4 *samboosay* but if you want to make more, simply increase the ingredients pro-rata. Any surplus can be frozen.

MAKES: 4 *samboosay*

Pastry and Flour and Water Paste
as on page 74

Filling
2 tablespoons hazel nuts, coarsely chopped

2 tablespoons pistachio nuts, coarsely chopped
2 sweet apples, finely chopped
caster sugar to taste
$\frac{1}{4}$ teaspoon ground green cardamom
icing sugar for dusting

1 Follow the method for samosas on page 74, using the filling given here.

2 After they have been deep fried, dust the *samboosay* with icing sugar and serve at once if you want them hot.

Am Ka Meetha

Mango Syllabub

The mango is indisputably the queen of the Indian fruit. Dozens of luscious species come into season at different times of the year and the best of them are exported to the West. They are quite a common sight now in the supermarket. This syllabub transforms them into a dessert which is effective, simple and unbelievably delicious.

SERVES: 4

2–3 fresh ripe sweet mangoes
8 oz (225 g) Greek or thick yoghurt
7 fl oz (200 ml) single cream

1 tablespoon milk powder
sugar to taste

1 Halve each mango, remove and discard the seed and scoop out the flesh. Discard the skin.

2 Combine all the ingredients in a food mixer and pulse into a purée.

3 Serve chilled.

Sri Lankan Fantasy

Exotic Fruit in Liquer and Syrup

Sri Lanka is home to many exotic fruit. Some are quite weird and distasteful to the Western palate. The custard apple and the guava, for example, do not please everyone at first taste.

I was once given the most wonderful Sri Lankan fruit salad, containing things I had never before encountered. It was bound together with *toddy*, the fiercely alcoholic native brew, and a divine syrup. In this version I use easily obtainable fruit and a combination of sweet sherry and vodka for the liquer, but you could use a combination of any exotic fruit available.

SERVES: 4   [V]

1 small whole pineapple
1 small melon
1 fresh mango
16 seedless grapes
4 bottled maraschino cherries

3 fl oz (75 ml) sweet (cream) sherry
2 fl oz (50 ml) vodka
sugar to taste
1 kiwi fruit

1 Prepare the pineapple by cutting off the top and bottom, cutting away the outer husks and the core, then dicing it into small cubes.

2 Halve the melon, discard the seeds then, using a melon scooper cut out melon balls.

3 Halve the mango, de-seed it and scrape out the flesh, cutting it into pieces.

4 Combine the above fruit along with the cherries and some of their juice, the sherry, vodka and sugar to taste.

5 Chill in the fridge for at least one hour.

6 Prior to serving, cut the skin off the kiwi fruit, slice it thinly and use the slices as a garnish.

Swinamakin

Sweet Semolina Pudding or Fudge

From Burma comes this simple-to-make, distinctive-tasting dessert. It can be eaten as a pudding of porridge-like consistency or, if baked, it becomes a type of fudge.

SERVES: 4

6 tablespoons ghee or sunflower oil
6 oz (150 g) semolina
4 tablespoons coconut milk powder
2 tablespoons caster sugar

$\frac{1}{2}$ teaspoon ground green cardamom
2 eggs
2 tablespoons shredded fresh or
    desiccated coconut

1 Heat the ghee or oil in a *karahi* or wok. Add the semolina and stir briskly for a couple of minutes.

2 Add water to the coconut milk powder to make a thick but easily pourable slurry.

3 Add it to the semolina and stir-fry for a further 3 or 4 minutes.

4 Add the sugar and cardamom and stir in.

5 If you want to serve it now as a hot pudding, add a little water (if needed) to get the consistency you require and serve. If you prefer to bake it and serve it cold, continue with the recipe.

6 Pre-heat the oven to 325°F/160°C Gas 3.

7 Separate the egg yolks and whites. Beat the whites into a foam. Add the yolks to the *karahi* and mix in. Follow with the egg whites.

8 Select an oven tray, about 8 inches (16 cm) square. Put aluminium foil on it and, evenly spread the mixture on it. Sprinkle the coconut on top.

9 Bake for 30 minutes then inspect. When it is a nice golden colour, remove from the oven and allow to cool.

10 When cold, cut into diamond shapes and serve.

Khao Niaw Man

Sticky Sweet Rice Balls

These marble-sized balls from Thailand are served cold. They are very easy to make, but you should use Thai or Japanese glutinous rice so that they hold together. The rice is naturally white, but it is traditional to colour some of the balls with green, red and yellow (sometimes even blue and purple) food colouring. The only effective way to achieve this is to use tartrazine food colours. These can be omitted if you have an aversion to them.

SERVES: 4   V

4 oz (110 g) glutinous rice
1 oz (30 g) coconut milk powder
½ teaspoon ground green cardamom
caster sugar to taste
food colouring if required
desiccated coconut

Syrup
¼ pint (150 ml) water
4 oz (110 g) caster sugar

1 Soak the rice for about 4 hours.

2 Bring a large pan of water to the boil.

3 Give the rice several cold water rinses until the water runs clear of starch.

4 Immerse the rice in hot water, then strain.

5 Add the rice to the boiling water in the pan. Stir it to ensure it is not sticking to the bottom of the pan, then let it boil for about 10–12 minutes.

6 Strain well then turn into a bowl and add the remaining ingredients apart from the syrup. Mix well.

7 If you want to colour the balls, divide the rice mixture into the number of colours you require, plus white, and while it is still warm add a different colour to each but one batch of rice. Allow to go completely cold.

8 Meanwhile make the syrup. Boil the water, add the sugar and boil until you get a thickish syrup.

9 Sprinkle desiccated coconut on to a work surface and roll out the mixture into balls, the size of your choice.

10 Place them in a serving bowl. Pour the syrup over the balls. Put in the fridge for 2–4 hours. Serve chilled.

Goreng Pisang

Banana Fritters

This recipe is immensely popular in Indonesia. You can buy piping-hot banana fritters anywhere from street stalls to high price restaurants and they are always superb. They are easy to make and the secret of this particular recipe is the use of custard powder and coconut milk powder to obtain its distinctive flavour.

SERVES: 4

6 small or 4 large ripe bananas
2 tablespoons custard powder
3 tablespoons cornflour
3 tablespoons coconut milk powder
1 egg

a few drops of vanilla essence
caster sugar, to taste
sunflower oil
icing sugar for dusting

1 Peel and mash the bananas.

2 Mix the custard powder, cornflour and coconut milk powder with the egg and the vanilla flavouring. Add just enough water to make a stiff batter. Add the sugar and the mashed banana, mixing well. The mixture should now drop off the spoon with a little resistence.

3 Heat a little oil in a large frying pan or a *tava*.

4 Spoon a dollop of mixture into the pan and flatten it a little with the back of the spoon. After 15–20 seconds make sure it is loose in the pan.

5 Repeat with further dollops, until the pan is full but not crammed full.

6 Turn the fritters after a couple of minutes, in the order they went in. Add oil as needed.

7 The size of your dollop will decide how many fritters you make and, of course, the size of your pan may mean cooking them in two or more batches.

8 As the fritters come out of the pan, dust with icing sugar and keep them warm until you serve them.

Appendix 1

THE CURRY CLUB

Pat Chapman always had a deep-rooted interest in spicy food, curry in particular, and over the years he built up a huge pool of information which he felt could be usefully passed on to others. He conceived the idea of forming an organisation for this purpose.

Since it was founded in January 1982, **The Curry Club** has built up a membership of several thousands. We have a marchioness, some lords and ladies, knights a-plenty, a captain of industry or two, generals, admirals and air marshals (not to mention a sprinkling of ex-colonels), and we have celebrity names – actresses, politicians, rock stars and sportsmen. We have an airline (Air India), a former R.N. warship (HMS *Hermes*) and a hotel chain (the Taj group). We have members on every continent and a good number of Asian members too. But by and large our membership is a typical cross-section of the Great British public, ranging in age from teenage to dotage, in occupation from refuse collectors to receivers. In fact thousands of people who have just one thing in common – a love of curry and spicy foods.

Members receive a bright and colourful magazine four times a year which has regular features on curry, the curry lands and other exotic and spicy cuisines. It includes news items, recipes, reports on restaurants, picture features and contributions from members and professionals alike.

The Club has produced a wide selection of publications, including this book and the others listed on page 2, all published by Piatkus. There is also a cookery video.

Obtaining ingredients required for Indian, Oriental and Middle Eastern cooking can be difficult but The Curry Club makes it easy with its well-established and efficient mail order service. Over 500 items are stocked, including spices, pickles, pastes, dried foods, canned foods, gift items, publications and specialist kitchen and table ware.

On the social side, the Club organises regular activities all over the UK. These include monthly 'nights' in London and specific 'nights' elsewhere, enabling members to meet the Club organisers, discuss specific queries, buy supplies and enjoy spicy snacks or meals. The Club also holds day and residential weekend cookery courses, gourmet nights to selected restaurants and similar enjoyable outings.

Top of the list are our regular Curry Club Gourmet Trips to India and other spicy countries. We take a small group of curry enthusiasts to the chosen country and tour the incredible sights, in between sampling the delicious foods of each region.

If you'd like to know more, write to **The Curry Club, P.O. Box 7, Haslemere, Surrey GU27 1EP   Telephone: 0428 658327.**

Appendix 2

THE STORE CUPBOARD

Here is a workable list of items you need to make the recipes in this book, subdivided into essential and non-essential. The essential items appear again and again in the recipes, the non-essential appear only in one or two. This list may look a bit formidable but remember, once you have the items in stock they will last for some time. I have listed in metric only as most of the packaging these days *is* metric only.

All items listed are available in the quantities stated, by post from The Curry Club.

ESSENTIAL WHOLE SPICES

Bay leaves	3 g
Cardamom, black or brown	30 g
Cardamom, green or white	30 g
Cassia bark	30 g
Chillies	11 g
Cloves	20 g
Coriander seeds	60 g
Cummin seeds, white	25 g
Curry leaves, dry	2 g
Fennel seeds	27 g
Fenugreek leaves, dry	18 g
Mustard seeds	65 g
Peppercorns, black	47 g
Sesame seeds, white	57 g
Wild onion seeds	47 g

NON-ESSENTIAL GROUND SPICES

Asafoetida	50 g
Cardamom, green	25 g
Cassia bark	25 g
Cloves	25 g
Galangale (Laos)	20 g
Lemon Grass (Serai)	20 g
Mango Powder	100 g

ESSENTIAL GROUND SPICES

Black pepper	100 g
Chilli powder	100 g
Coriander	100 g
Cummin	100 g
Garam masala	50 g
Garlic powder and/or flakes	100 g
Ginger	100 g
Paprika	100 g
Turmeric	100 g

ESSENTIAL DRY FOODS

Basmati rice	2 kg
Coconut Powder	100 g
Gram flour	1 kg
Masoor (red) lentils	500 g

NON-ESSENTIAL WHOLE SPICES

Alkenet root	3 g
Cinnamon bark	6 pieces
Cummin seeds, black	25 g
Dill seeds	25 g
Fenugreek seeds	47 g
Ginger, dried	6 pieces
Lovage seeds	27 g
Mace	8 g
Nutmeg, whole	6 nuts
Panch phoran	30 g
Pomegranate seeds	30 g
Poppy seeds	52 g
Saffron stamens	½ g

NON-ESSENTIAL DRY FOODS

Food colouring powder, red (beetroot powder)	25 g
Food colouring powder, yellow (annatto)	25 g
Lentils –	
Channa, split	500 g
Moong green, whole	500 g
Toor or tovar, split	500 g
Urid, whole black	500 g
Nuts –	
Almond, whole	50 g
Almond, ground	100 g
Cashew	100 g
Peanuts, raw	100 g
Pistachio	100 g
Papadoms, spiced and plain (pack)	300 g
Puffed rice (mamra)	100 g
Red kidney beans	500 g
Rice flour	500 g
Rose water, bottle	7 fl oz
Sev (gram flour snack)	200 g
Silver leaf (edible)	6 sheets
Supari mixture	100 g
Tamarind block	300 g

Glossary

A

Achar – Pickle

Adrak – Ginger

Ajwain or Ajowain – Lovage seeds

Akhni – Spicy consommé – like stock. Also called *yakni*

Allspice – Native to the West Indies. Related to the clove family, the seed resembles small dried peas. Called allspice because its aroma seems to combine those of clove, cinnamon, ginger, nutmeg and pepper. Used rather more in Middle Eastern cooking than Indian

Aloo – Potato

Am – Mango

Am chur – Mango powder

Anardana – Pomegranate

Aniseed – *Saunf.* Small deliciously flavoured seeds resembling fennel seeds

Areca – Betel nut

Asafoetida – *Hing.* Gum obtained from root of giant fennel-like plant. Used in powder or resin form. A rather smelly spice

Ata or Atta – *Chupatti* flour. Fine wholemeal flour used in most Indian breads. English wholemeal is a suitable alternative

B

Badain – Star anise

Badam – Almond

Bargar – The process of frying whole spices in hot oil

Basil – Used only in religious applications in Indian cooking, but widely in Thai cooking

Basmati – The best type of long-grain rice

Bay leaf – This very well known leaf is used fresh or dried in certain Indian recipes

Besan – see *Gram flour*

Bhajee or Bhaji – Dryish mild vegetable curry

Bhajia – Deep-fried fritter, usually onion. See *Pakora*

Bhare – Stuffed

Bharta or Bhurta – Mash or purée

Bhoona or Bhuna – The process of cooking the spice paste in hot oil. A *bhoona* curry is usually dry and cooked in coconut

Bhunana – Roast

Bindi – Okra or lady's fingers

Biriani – Traditionally rice baked with meat or vegetable filling with saffron, served with edible silver foil. The restaurant interpretation is a fried rice artificially coloured, with filling added

Black salt – *Kala namak.* A type of salt, dark grey in colour. Its taste, of sea water, is relished in India but not, I find, in the West

Brinjal – Aubergine

Burfi or Barfi – An Indian fudge-like sweetmeat made from reduced condensed milk in various flavours eg plain or pistachio (green)

C

Cardamom – *Elaichi.* One of the most aromatic and expensive spices. It is a pod containing slightly sticky black seeds. There are three main types: *Brown* (also called black) have a rather hairy, husky, dark brown casing about 20 mm long. Used in garam masala, kormas and pullaos. Quite pungent. *Green* have a smooth, pale green outer casing about 10 mm long. Used whole or ground, with or without casing in many savoury and sweet recipes. *White* are about the same size as green with a slightly rounder white casing. Green and white have a similar flavour – more delicate than the brown

Cashew nuts – *Kaju*

Cassia bark – A corky bark with a sweet fragrance similar to cinnamon. Cassia is coarser and cooks better than cinnamon and is used extensively in northern Indian cookery. Although cooked in the curry the bark is too coarse to eat

Cayenne pepper – A blend of chilli powder from Latin America

Ceylon Curry – Usually cooked with coconut, lemon and chilli

Chakla belan – Special rolling pin and board

Chamcha – Ladle

Chana – Type of lentil. See *Dhal*

Chawal – Rice

Chhalni – Sieve

Chilli – There are a great many species of chillies, which are the fleshy pods of shrub-like bushes of the capsicum family. Chillies range from large to small, and colours include green, white, purple, pink and red. Curiously, although synonymous with Indian food they were only brought to the sub-continent from South America some four centuries ago. They are now the most important heat agent in Indian cookery. They vary in hotness from mild to incendiary-like potency. Most commonly, small green or red chillies are used fresh. Red chillies can be dried and used whole, and chilli powder is made by grinding dried chillies

Chupatti – A dry 6 inch (15 cm) disc of unleavened bread. Normally griddle cooked, it should be served piping hot. Spelling varies eg *Chuppati*, *Chapati* etc

Chutneys – The common ones are onion, mango and *tandoori*. There are dozens of others which rarely appear on the standard menu. See *Sambals*

Cinnamon – *Dalchini*. The quill-like dried bark of the cinnamon tree. It is one of the most aromatic spices. Same family as cassia, it is generally used in dishes which require a delicate flavour

Cloves – *Lavang*. The most familiar spice in the UK where it has been continuously used since Roman times. Expensive and fragrant, it is an unopened flower bud

Colcasia – A tuber, also called *taro*

Coriander – *Dhania*. One of the most important spices in Indian cookery. The leaves of the plant can be used fresh and the seeds used whole or ground

Cummin or Cumin – *Jeera*. There are two types of seeds: *white* and *black*. The white seeds are a very important spice in Indian cookery. The black seeds (*kala jeera*) are nice in pullao rice and certain vegetable dishes. Both can be used whole or ground

Curry – The only word in this glossary to have no direct translation into any of the sub-continent's fifteen or so languages. The work was coined by the British in India centuries ago. Possible contenders for the origin of the word are, *karahi* or *karai* (Hindi), a wok-like frying-pan used all over India to prepare masalas (spice mixtures), *karhi*, a soup-like dish made with spices, gram flour dumplings and buttermilk, *kari*, a spicy Tamil sauce. Turkuri, a seasoned sauce or stew, or *kari phulia*, *neem* or curry leaves. *Kudhi* or *kadhi*, a yoghurt soup, or *koresh*, an aromatic Iranian stew

Curry lands – India is the main curry land with 600 million, mainly Hindu, people. Other curry lands are her Moslem neighbours to the west – Pakistan, Afghanistan, and, to a lesser extent, Iran which is the root of some Indian food. To the north lie Nepal and Bhutan whilst Moslem Bangladesh lies to the east. India's south eastern curry-land neighbours include the predominantly Buddhist Burma and Thailand, whilst multinational Malaysia and Singapore, with huge, mainly Moslem Indian populations are also curry lands. The tiny island of Sri Lanka has a very distinctive curry style and one must not forget significant pockets of curry eating Asians in Africa and the Caribbean. The total number of people whose 'staple' diet is curry exceeds 1 billion people – 25 per cent of the world's population.

Curry leaves – *Neem* leaves or *kari phulia*. Small leaves a bit like bay leaves, used for flavouring

D

Dahi – Yoghurt

182

Dalchini or Darchim – Cinnamon

Degchi, Dekhchi or Degh – Brass or metal saucepan without handles also called *Pateeli* or *batloi*

Dewa – Wooden spoon

Dhal – Lentils. There are over sixty types of lentil in the sub-continent, some of which are very obscure. Like peas, they grow into a hard sphere measuring between 10 mm (chickpeas) and 3 mm (urid). They are cooked whole or split with skin, or split with it polished off. Lentils are a rich source of protein and when cooked with spices are extremely tasty. The common types are *chana* (resembling yellow split peas, used to make gram flour/besam; *kabli chana* (chickpeas); *masoor* (the most familiar orangey-red lentil which has a green skin); *moong* (green skin lentil, used also to make bean sprouts); *toor*, or *toovar* (dark yellow and very oily); and *urid* (black skin, white lentil)

Dhania – Coriander

Dhansak – Traditional Parsee dish cooked in a purée of lentils, aubergine, tomato and spinach. Some restaurants also add pineapple pieces

Dhungar – Applying the smoke of charcoal to ingredients

Doroo – Celery

Dosa or Dosai – A South Indian pancake made from rice and lentil flour. Usually served with a filling

Dum – Steam cooking. Long before the West invented the pressure cooker, India had her own method which lasts to this day. A pot with a close fitting lid is sealed with a ring of dough. The ingredients are then cooked in their own steam under some pressure

E

Ekuri – Spiced scrambled eggs

Elaichi – Cardamom

F

Fennel – *Sonf* or *soonf*. A small green seed which is very aromatic, with aniseed taste. Delicious in pullao rice

Fenugreek – *Methi*. This important spice is used as seeds and in fresh or dried leaf form. It is very savoury and is used in many Northern Indian dishes

Five Spice powder – Combination of five sweet and aromatic spices used in Chinese and Malay cooking. Usually ground. A typical combination would be equal parts of cinnamon, cloves, fennel seeds, star anise and szechuan pepper

Foogath – Lightly cooked vegetable dish

G

Gajar – Carrot

Galingale or Galangel – A tuber related to ginger which comes in varieties called greater or lesser. It has a more peppery taste than ginger (which can be substituted for it). It is used in Thai cooking where it is called *kha*, and in Indonesian (*laos*) and Malay (*kenkur*). It is available in the UK in fresh form (rare), dried or powdered

Garam masala – Literally hot mixture. This refers to a blend of spices much loved in northern Indian cookery. Curry Club garam masala contains nine spices

Garlic – *Lasan*

Ghee – Clarified butter or margarine much used in northern Indian cookery

Ginger – *Adrak* (fresh), *sont* (dried), a rhizome which can be used fresh, dried or powdered

Gobi or Phoolgobi – Cauliflower

Goor or Gur – Jaggery (palm sugar) or molasses

Gram flour – *Besan*. Finely ground flour, pale blonde in colour, made from chana (see *Dhal*). Used to make *pakoras* and to thicken curries

H

Handi – Earthenware cooking pot

Hindi – Hindi is the official language of India. Although there are fourteen or so other languages in India, only Hindi translations have been used in this glossary. Spelling of Hindi words can vary in English because they are translated phonetically from many Hindi dialects

Hing – Asafoetida

Hisa – Bill (account)

Huldi – Turmeric

I

Imli – Tamarind

J

Jaifal or Taifal – Nutmeg

Jaggery – see *Goor*
Javatri – Mace
Jeera or Zeera – Cummin

K

Kabli chana – Chickpeas. See *Dhal*
Kaju – Cashew nut
Kala – Black
Kala jeera – Black cummin seeds
Kala namak – Black salt
Karahi – *Karai, korai* etc. Indian two handled cooking *karahi*; the Indian equivalent of the wok. The *karahi* is a circular two handled round all-purpose cooking pan used for stir-frying, simmering, frying and deep-frying – in fact it is highly efficient for all types of cooking. Some restaurants cook in small *karahis* and serve them straight to the table with the food sizzling inside
Kashmir curry – Restaurateurs' creation. A sweetish curry often using lychees or similar ingredient
Katori – Small serving bowls which go on a *thali* (tray)
Kecap manis – Indonesian version of soy sauce. It is sweeter and slightly sticky. Soy sauce is a good, though more salty substitute
Kewra – Screwpine water. An extract of the flower of the tropical screwpine tree. It is a fragrant clear liquid used to flavour sweets. It is a cheap substitute for rose water
Kish mish – Sultanas
Kofta – Minced vegetable balls in batter, deep-fried, and then cooked in a curry sauce

L

Lasan – Garlic
Lassi or Lhassi – A refreshing drink made from yoghurt and crushed ice. The savoury version is *lhassi namkeen* and the sweet version is *lhassi meethi*
Lavang – Cloves
Lemon Grass – Takrai (Thai), serai (Malay). A fragrant leafed plant which imparts a subtle lemony flavour to cooking. Use ground powder (made from the bulb) as a substitute
Lentils – see *Dhal*
Lovage – *Ajwain* or *ajowain*. Slightly bitter round seeds

M

Mace – *Javitri*. The outer part of the nutmeg
Madras – You will not find a traditional recipe for Madras curry.... It is another restaurateurs' invention. But the people of South India *do* eat hot curries; some original chef must have christened his hot curry 'Madras' and the name stuck
Makke – Cornflour
Malai – Cream
Malaya – The curries of Malaya are traditionally cooked with plenty of coconut, chilli and ginger. In the Indian restaurant, however, they are usually mild and contain pineapple and other fruit
Mamra – Puffed *basmati* rice
Mango Powder – *Am chur*. A very sour flavouring agent
Masala – A mixture of spices which are cooked with a particular dish. Any curry powder is therefore a masala. It can be spelt a remarkable number of ways – massala, massalla, musala, mosola, massalam etc
Masoor – Red lentils. See *Dhal*
Mattar – Green peas
Meethi – Sweet
Methi – Fenugreek
Mirch – Pepper or chilli
Moglai or Moghlai – Cooking in the style of the Moghul emperors whose chefs took Indian cookery to the heights of gourmet cuisine three centuries ago. Few restaurateurs who offer Moglai dishes come anywhere near this excellence. True Moglai dishes are expensive and time-consuming to prepare authentically. Can also be variously spelt muglai, mogulai, moglai etc
Mooli – Large white radish
Moong – Type of lentil. See *Dahl*
Munacca – Raisins
Mustard seed – Small black seeds which become sweetish when fried. Yellow variety used to make English mustard to which flour and colouring is added

N

Namak – Salt
Namkeen – Salty
Naan or Nan – Leavened bread baked in the *tandoor*. It is teardrop shaped and about 8–10 inches (20–25 cm) long. It must be served fresh and hot
Naan, Peshwari – Naan bread stuffed with

almonds and or cashew and/or raisins and baked in the *tandoor*

Naryal – Coconut

Neem – Curry leaf

Nimboo – Lime (lemon)

Nutmeg – *Jaifal*

O

Okra – *Bindi*. A pulpy vegetable also known as lady's fingers

P

Pakoras – To all intents and purposes the same as the *bhajia*

Palak or Sag – Spinach

Panch Phoran – Five seeds. A mixture of five spices used in Bengali vegetable cooking, comprising equal amounts of cummin, fennel, fenugreek, mustard and wild onion seeds

Paneer – Cheese made from bottled milk which can be fried and curried (*mattar paneer*)

Papadom – Thin lentil flour wafers. When cooked (deep fried or baked) they expand to about 8 inches (20 cm). They must be crackling crisp and warm when served. If not send them back to be re-heated and deduct points from that restaurant. They come plain or spiced with lentils, pepper, garlic or chilli. Many spelling variations include popodom, pappodom etc

Paprika – Mild red ground pepper made from red capsicum peppers. It originally came from Hungary and only reached India this century. Its main use is to give red colour to a dish

Paratha – A deep-fried bread

Patna – A long-grained rice

Pepper – *Mirch*. Has for centuries been India's most important spice, gaining it the title 'king of spices'. It grows on vines which flower triennially and produce clusters of berries, which are picked and dried and become the peppercorns. Green, black and white pepper are not different varieties. All peppercorns are green when picked and must be bottled or freeze-dried at once to retain the colour. Black pepper is the dried berry. White pepper is obtained by soaking off the black skin of the berry. Peppercorns are a heat agent and can be used whole or ground

Phal or Phall – A very hot curry (the hottest) invented by restaurateurs

Piaz, Peeaz or Pyaz – Onion

Pickles – Pungent, hot pickled vegetables or meat essential to an Indian meal. Most common are lime, mango and chilli

Pistachio nut – *Pista magaz*. A fleshy, tasty nut which can be used fresh (the greener the better) or salted. It is expensive and goes well in savoury or sweet dishes such as *biriani* or *pista kulfi* (ice cream)

Podina – Mint leaves or powder

Pullao – Rice and meat or vegetables cooked together in a pan until tender. In many restaurants the ingredients are mixed after cooking to save time (see also **Biriani**)

Pullao rice – The restaurant name for rice fried with spices and coloured yellow

Pulses – Types of lentils

Puri – A deep-fried unleavened bread about 4 inches (10 cm) in diameter. It puffs up when cooked and should be served at once

R

Rai – Mustard seed

Raita – A cooling chutney of yoghurt and vegetable, cucumber for instance, which accompanies the main meal

Rajma – Red kidney beans

Rose water – *Ruh gulab*. A clear essence extracted from rose petals to give fragrance to sweets. See *Kewra*

Roti – Bread

Ruh gulab – Rose water essence

S

Sabzi – A generic term for vegetables

Saffron – *Kesar* or *zafron*. The world's most expensive spice, saffron is the stigma of the crocus flower. A few stigmas are all that are needed to give a recipe a delicate yellow colouring and aroma

Sag or Saag – Spinach

Salt – *Namak*

Sambals – A Malayan term describing the side dishes accompanying the meal. Sometimes referred to on the Indian menu

Sambar – A South Indian vegetable curry made largely from lentils

Samosa – The celebrated triangular deep-fried meat or vegetable patties served as starters or snacks

Sarson ka sag – Mustard leaves (spinach-like)

Saunf or Souf – Aniseed

Seenl – Allspice

Sesame seed – *Til*. Small round discs, the white species are widely used in Indian cooking, the black in Chinese

Sil batta – A pair of grinding stones: *sil*, large stone, *batta*, small pounder

Sonf – Fennel seed

Sont or Sonth – Dry ginger

Star Anise – A pretty star-shaped spice used in Chinese Five Spices, and it is lovely in pullao rice

Sub-continent – Term to describe India, Pakistan, Bangladesh, Nepal, Burma, and Sri Lanka as a group

Supari – Mixture of seeds and sweeteners for chewing after a meal. Usually includes aniseed or fennel, shredded betel nut, sugar balls, marrow seeds etc

T

Taipal or Jaiphal – Nutmeg.

Tamarind – *Imli*. A date-like fruit used as a chutney, and in cooking as a souring agent

Tarka – Garnish of spices/onion

Tarka dhal – Lentils garnished with fried spices

Tava or Tawa – A heavy almost flat, circular wooden handled griddle pan used to cook Indian breads and to 'roast' spices. Also ideal for many cooking functions from frying eggs and omelettes to making pancakes etc

Tej patia – The leaf of the cassia bark tree. Resembles bay leaf which can be used in its place

Thali sets – To serve your meal in truly authentic Indian fashion use *thali* sets. A great and stylish talking point. Each diner is served a *thali* tray on which is a number of *katori* dishes in which different curry dishes, rice, chutneys, etc. are placed. Breads and papadoms go on the tray itself

Til – Sesame seed

Toor or Toovar – A type of lentil. See *Dhal*.

Turmeric – *Haldi* or *huldi*. A very important Indian spice, turmeric is a rhizome. The fresh root is used occasionally as a vegetable or in pickles. The ground spice is extensively used to give the familiar yellow colour to curries. Use sparingly or it can cause bitterness.

Tusei – Basil

U

Udrak – Ginger

Urid – A type of lentil. See *Dahl*

V

Vark or Varak – Edible silver or gold foil

Y

Yakni – see *Akhni*

Z

Zafron – Saffron

Zeera – Cummin

Index